What's Your Evidence?

Engaging K–5 Students in Constructing Explanations in Science

What's Your Evidence?

Engaging K–5 Students in Constructing Explanations in Science

Carla Zembal-Saul

The Pennsylvania State University

Katherine L. McNeill

Boston College

Kimber Hershberger

State College Area School District

PEARSON

Boston   Columbus   Indianapolis   New York   San Francisco   Upper Saddle River
Amsterdam   Cape Town   Dubai   London   Madrid   Milan   Munich   Paris   Montreal   Toronto
Delhi   Mexico City   São Paulo   Sydney   Hong Kong   Seoul   Singapore   Taipei   Tokyo

Senior Acquisitions Editor: Kelly Villella Canton
Vice President, Editor in Chief: Aurora Martinez Ramos
Editorial Assistant: Annalea Manalili
Executive Marketing Manager: Krista Clark
Project Manager: Karen Mason
Manufacturing Buyer: Megan Cochran
Text Designer: Element LLC
Manager, Rights and Permissions: Tim Nicholls
Image Permission Coordinator: Annie Pickert
Manager, Cover Visual Research & Permissions: Diane Lorenzo
Cover Designer: Jenny Hart
Cover Art: Photo by: Tina Hoeltmann
Interior Photos: Photos of Carla Zember-Saul and Kimber Hershberger: Heidi Lewis/Heidi Lynne Photography; Photo of Katherine McNeill: Media Technology Services, Boston College; interior photos by Tina Hoeltmann, Judi Kur, and Carla Zembal-Saul
Media Director: Sacha Laustsen
Full-Service Project Management: Element LLC
Composition: Element LLC
Printer/Binder: RR Donnelley & Sons

[CIP data not available at time of publication.]

10 9 8 7 6 5 4

ISBN-10: 0-13-211726-6
ISBN-13: 978-0-13-211726-5

We dedicate this book to "young scientists" everywhere, especially Zach and Thomas. May you always keep your sense of wonder about the world and how it works.

We also dedicate this book to our spouses, Jerry, Ryan, and John, respectively, for their persistent encouragement, unwavering support, and love.

About the Authors

Carla Zembal-Saul is a professor of science education in the College of Education at The Pennsylvania State University. She holds the Kahn Professorship in STEM Education and currently serves as head of the Department of Curriculum and Instruction. A former middle school science teacher, Zembal-Saul earned her doctorate at the University of Michigan. She has been involved in school–university partnership work for more than fifteen years, and most of her teaching, scholarship, and service take place in that context. Her research focuses on K–6 teacher learning as they engage in professional development aimed at supporting students in talking and writing evidence-based arguments in science. Examining classroom discourse is a fundamental aspect of her work, and she employs video analysis as both a research tool and a pedagogical approach for working with teachers. Zembal-Saul has published her research findings in numerous book chapters and articles in peer-reviewed journals, and she is active in professional organizations, including the NARST and National Science Teachers Association.

Katherine L. McNeill is an assistant professor of science education at Boston College. A former middle school science teacher, she received her doctorate in science education from the University of Michigan. Her research focuses on how to support students with diverse backgrounds in engaging in scientific explanation and argumentation in both talk and writing. Her research has been generously funded by the National Science Foundation (NSF). From this work, she has published a book on engaging middle school students in scientific explanation, numerous book chapters, and articles in a variety of journals, including the *Journal of Research in*

Science Teaching, Science Education, the *Journal of the Learning Sciences,* and the *International Journal of Science Education.* In 2011, McNeill received the Early Career Research Award from NARST. She has also conducted numerous workshops at the annual meeting of the National Science Teachers Association and for various school districts, including the Detroit Public Schools and the Boston Public Schools.

Kimber Hershberger is currently a third-grade teacher in the State College Area School District (SCASD) in Pennsylvania. She also serves a co-instructor for the science methods course and a mentor teacher for the Penn State–SCASD Professional Development School Partnership. Her involvement in a local professional learning community that focuses on incorporating content storyline and the CER framework in science teaching has been a highlight of her work. She holds degrees from Juniata College (B.S., elementary education) and The Pennsylvania State University (M.Ed., science education). She has co-authored several articles for NSTA journals, including *Science and Children* and *Science Scope.* In addition, Hershberger has presented numerous times at the annual conference of the National Science Teachers Association, including sessions at the Research Dissemination Conference, about her work on how to scaffold students' use of claims and evidence through science talks and notebooks.

Contents

xii

Contents

Video Contents

Foreword

As the principal and lead learner of Park Forest Elementary School in State College Area School District and as a strong advocate for science, I have an investment in helping students become global citizens who understand science. I strongly believe that guiding our students to think like scientists and participate in scientific practices is an important task for our teachers. At a time when many schools and districts are concerned primarily about reading and math scores in order to make adequate yearly progress, it is imperative that we find time and opportunity to engage students in meaningful science learning. Talking and writing about science is an important way for students to increase their language skills. Language skills used in science discourse are critical if our students are to become competent, discerning, and active scholars who can be instruments of change in our world. Asking students to verbalize and write their science explanations using claims, evidence, and reasoning engages students in productive inquiry and language practices that require them to think more deeply about science concepts and how to apply them in everyday life.

Although my school has a number of students with learning challenges, I have observed that science is a subject that levels the playing field. All children have a natural sense of wonder and excitement about science and the world. As children investigate and experience science lessons, they contribute equally because of the engaging and interactive nature of instruction. When teachers gather students for science talks following investigation, all of the students can participate in the discussions because they can share firsthand knowledge of the concepts. English language learners who are just beginning to use English are able to demonstrate what they found using the materials or by showing their science journal illustrations.

As I read this book by Carla Zembal-Saul, Katherine McNeill, and Kimber Hershberger, I was excited to find a resource that will help both experienced and beginning teachers to think about their science teaching practices. I hope to use the book in a lesson study group with my teachers so they can support each other as they identify ways to teach using coherent content storylines and scientific explanations. I love that teachers can look at video clips and share their observations in order to learn from other teachers about ways they can adapt the science talks. The study questions are perfect for guiding conversations in ways that allow teachers to examine their own practices, implement change, and reflect on their progress with each other.

Argumentation and discourse are essential components of science communities. This book encourages teachers to become comfortable with questioning and guiding conversations between children who agree and disagree. Respectful listening and conversations are an important element of scientific investigations. Providing students with the opportunity to engage in discourse practices will carry over as a life-long learning skill that is essential in a democracy.

I highly endorse this book and the practices it promotes for science explanations and discourse. As a learning tool for teachers, it will truly enhance the way they guide children to think, participate, and talk like scientists. Additionally, if used to support a study group or professional learning community, the dialogue between teachers could impact the whole school to become a science community.

Donnan Stoicovy
Principal/Lead Learner
Park Forest Elementary School
State College, PA

Preface

Although there has long been acknowledgment that learning both content and processes are important aspects of school science, new views of proficiency in science today emphasize engaging learners in scientific practices (Duschl, Schweingruber, & Shouse, 2007; Michaels, Shouse, & Schweingruber, 2008; National Research Council [NRC] 2011). Not only should students understand and be able to apply scientific ideas to explain natural phenomena but they also should be able to generate and evaluate scientific evidence, construct and debate evidence-based explanations, and participate productively in a community of science learners. It was once thought that young children were not yet capable of the sophisticated reasoning necessary to participate in these complex practices, but recent research on children's thinking (and our own experiences in classrooms) suggests that they can become quite competent at engaging in scientific reasoning and practices (Duschl et al., 2007). In this book, we embrace a view of children as capable young scientists and we approach the teaching of science in ways that nurture their innate curiosity about how the natural world works. We also provide specific research-based approaches intended to support all K–5 children in talk and writing associated with constructing scientific explanations.

The benefits of engaging students in constructing scientific explanations is well established. Our research has shown that when students write and analyze scientific explanations, there is a positive impact on their ability to use evidence, justify claims, and reason scientifically (McNeill, in press; McNeill, Lizotte, Krajcik & Marx, 2006; McNeill & Krajcik, 2009). In addition, when students construct scientific explanations, they learn important science concepts (Bell & Linn, 2000; McNeill et al., 2006; McNeill & Krajcik, 2009; Zohar & Nemet, 2002). Students also develop twenty-first century skills, such as communication and problem solving, which are important for career readiness (Krajcik & Sutherland, 2009). Finally, this approach facilitates the intentional connection between science and literacy, which a number of educators have argued can enhance the learning of both (Hand, 2008; Hand & Keys, 1999). When students are engaged in constructing, communicating, and critiquing scientific explanations, they make their thinking public (Bell & Linn, 2000; Michaels et al., 2008). After that thinking has been made visible, peers can consider whether their understandings are consistent with or different from the ideas of their classmates, and teachers can monitor and assess student learning. Note that in this book we purposefully point out the ways in which strategies and scaffolds can be used to support all students to develop proficiency in science, including English language learners (ELLs) and students with special needs.

In our work, we acknowledge that teaching in this way can be challenging. We think of teachers as nothing short of super-heroes as they reconsider their practice and attempt new approaches in the classroom. Our research and experiences clearly indicate that teachers are pivotal with respect to how they integrate the instructional strategies described in this book (Zembal-Saul, 2009). This is especially true in terms of whether key benefits, such as deepening students' science content understandings and improving their abilities to develop evidence-based explanations, are realized (McNeill, 2009; McNeill & Krajcik, 2009). Therefore, our approach is to provide a framework for explanation that educators can use to organize everything from planning to instructional strategies and from scaffolds to assessment. Moreover, students also can use the scientific explanation framework to inform their science talk and writing.

The framework is based on our research on scientific explanation (McNeill et al., 2006) and argument (Zembal-Saul, 2005, 2007, 20095) and variations of it have been used with teachers for more than a decade. The framework for scientific explanation consists of making a *claim* and using *evidence* and *reasoning* to support it, which is why we often refer to it as the *CER framework*. Not only does the CER framework address having students learn scientific explanations but it also teaches students how to construct explanations from evidence and how to evaluate those explanations. The framework is built on national standards and reform documents in science education, including the *National Science Education Standards* (NRC, 1996), *Benchmarks for Scientific Literacy* (AAAS, 1993), *Taking Science to School* (Duschl et al., 2007), *Ready, Set, Science!* (Michaels et al., 2008), and *A Framework for K–12 Science Education: Practices, Crosscutting Concepts, and Core Ideas* (NRC, 2011), as well as national standards in literacy around argumentation and persuasion, including the Common Core Standards for English Language Arts (Common Core State Standards Initiative, 2010).

For many teachers, engaging students in constructing scientific explanations is a marked departure from the way they typically teach science. The teachers we have had the privilege of working with over the years frequently remark that although learning the approach is challenging, the benefits are rewarding and they cannot imagine teaching science any other way. To successfully implement the CER framework and associated strategies in your classroom, these teachers recommend working with at least one colleague, attempting new strategies in small manageable chunks, and being patient with yourself and with your students as you work to establish norms for talking and writing scientific explanations. We think this is good advice and hope that *What's Your Evidence?* supports you on your journey to improve the teaching of science for all children.

Key Features of The Book

Throughout this book, we utilize six key features to discuss and illustrate strategies for integrating scientific explanation into elementary classrooms.

- Each chapter begins with a *vignette* that provides a scenario from an elementary classroom that illustrates the key points that we discuss throughout the chapter. The goal of the vignettes is to provide a vision for what the essential ideas look like in practice.
- Within the chapters, we integrate samples of ***students' written work*** from actual elementary students to show strong examples as well as common student difficulties with scientific explanations across the grade levels.
- To illustrate both student talk and various teacher instructional strategies we use *video clips* from elementary classrooms. These video clips include a range of grade levels to demonstrate scientific explanations at varying levels of complexity and different science topics to show what they can look like in different domains.
- Integrated into the chapters are ***strategies to support all students*** in constructing scientific explanations in both talk and writing, including students with a range of backgrounds and experiences, such as English language learners and students with special needs.
- At the end of each chapter, we include a ***check point*** that provides a synthesis of the key points discussed in the chapter and foreshadows what will be discussed in future chapters. The check points provide a road map of the essential ideas in the book.
- Each chapter also ends with ***study group questions***, which can either be used individually or with a group of colleagues to reflect on and apply the key ideas discussed in the chapter to actual elementary classrooms.

Our goal is that by the end of reading this book, you will have a clear image of what it looks like to incorporate scientific explanations into both talk and writing at the elementary level. Furthermore, you will have a variety of strategies and tools in order to support you in integrating scientific explanations in your own classroom to foster a community of young scientists.

Overview of the Chapters

The first two chapters of *What's Your Evidence?* provide an overview and justification for explanation-driven science instruction. Chapter 1 provides a rationale for the importance of focusing on scientific explanation in grades K–5, including a discussion of alignment with national standards and reform documents. In this chapter, we use examples of students' written work and science talks to illustrate what scientific explanation looks like in elementary classrooms. In Chapter 2, we introduce the scientific explanation framework (i.e., claim, evidence, reasoning, and rebuttal) and discuss how the framework can be used to support all students in science writing and science talk. We provide multiple examples of the framework across science content areas and grade levels, as well as discuss different variations of the framework, which can be adapted based on the age, experience, and background of students.

In the next three chapters, we describe how to design instruction that provides opportunities and appropriate supports to engage all students in scientific explanations. Chapter 3 focuses on planning for explanation-driven science instruction, including developing a coherent science content storyline that emphasizes the central ideas in science, builds logically over time, and provides opportunities for scientific explanation. Furthermore, the chapter discusses two essential features to consider when identifying opportunities in the curriculum for scientific explanation learning tasks, as well as ways to modify learning tasks to make them more or less complex to meet the needs of your students. Chapter 4 describes different supports for engaging all students in scientific talk and writing. Specifically, the chapter discusses the dynamic interplay between talking and writing, scaffolding moves for scientific talk, and visual representations and other prompts for scientific writing. In Chapter 5, we continue to illustrate ways to integrate scientific explanations into K–5 classrooms. We describe an instructional sequence that provides students with opportunities for constructing scientific explanations, as well as a variety of instructional strategies that can be valuable tools for teachers as they work with their elementary students.

The final two chapters focus on student assessment and providing support both for students and for teachers over time. Chapter 6 explains how to design and use student assessments to inform instruction. We describe a five-step process for developing assessment tasks and rubrics, as well as discuss how to use assessment data to modify instruction to better meet the needs of all students. The final chapter centers on how to foster a community of young scientists over time, as well as how to support your journey as a teacher to change science teaching practices. In terms of fostering a community of young scientists, we describe norms of participation, such as actively listening, patterns of talk, and a culture of constructive criticism, that help facilitate this process. Furthermore, we share comments from the elementary teachers with whom we have worked. These dedicated educators have provided reflections on the rewards and challenges of teaching science by way of scientific explanations, as well as recommendations on how to rethink and change your practice over time.

About the Video

All the video clips associated with this text were filmed in elementary grade classrooms in central, rural Pennsylvania. None of the lessons was staged or scripted. The video was not professionally recorded or produced, given that our aim was to be as nonintrusive as possible in the classrooms in which we were guests. Permissions were secured for all students and teachers appearing in the video clips. We hope those who view the videos are as grateful as we are that these teachers were willing to share their attempts to integrate scientific explanation into their science teaching practices, providing us with insights that would not be possible without the videos. These teachers are the true heroes of this work.

Acknowledgments

This book would not have been possible without our teacher collaborators whose commitment to improving the teaching and learning of science for all students inspired us to take on the project. Over the years we have worked with numerous teachers who welcomed us into their classrooms, allowed us to co-teach and try out our ideas, bravely attempted new practices while we video recorded them (and agreed to share their teaching with others), and provided valuable insights and feedback that informed the work. They are the true heroes of change. In particular, we thank the State College Area School District professional learning community teachers who read and commented on numerous drafts of this book and openly shared their journeys of innovation with us: Jennifer Cody, Jessica Cowan, Liz Cullin, Jennifer Grube, M. J. Kitt, and Judi Kur. Penn State University science education graduate students Alicia McDyre and Mark Merritt also provided important feedback and editing support throughout the process, as did local principals Deirdre Bauer and Donnan Stoicovy. We are also grateful to thank the science department and the numerous elementary teachers we have worked with in the Boston Public Schools who have shared their successes, challenges, and strategies around scientific explanation. In particular, we thank Pam Pelletier for her districtwide support as well as Dean Martin and Erik Roberts for sharing their creative supports for science writing.

The original ideas and research around which this book was written were drawn in part from several projects funded by the National Science Foundation—TESSA: Teaching Elementary School Science as Argument (NSF REC 0237922) and Supporting Grade 5–8 Students in Writing Scientific Explanations (DRL-0836099). Any opinions, findings, conclusions, or recommendations expressed in this material are those of the authors and do not necessarily reflect the views of the National Science Foundation. We are grateful for NSF's generous support of our work and the opportunity to share findings with teachers in a way that has the potential to impact what happens in classrooms.

We would like to thank the reviewers who took the time to read our manuscript and provide valuable feedback: Reizelie Barreto-Espino, Towson University; Dorene V. Calvin, Anna M. Rudy Elementary; Jennifer Lynn Cody, Park Forest Elementary School, State College Area School District; Ann Hardy, Vermilion Parish School Board; Laura Hill, District School Board of Pasco County; Kaitlyn

Hood, Perkins Academy; Patricia Kincaid, Denver Public Schools; Linda J. Morris, Denver Public Schools; Paul W. Nance, Jordan School District; Gary R. Peterson, North Clackamas School District; Lisa N. Pitot, Poudre School District; Sharon F. Shrum, Frederick County Virginia Public Schools; Donnan M. Stoicovy, Park Forest Elementary School; Jeannine Tantalo, Laurelton-Pardee School, East Irondequoit Central School District; Sara Torres, Columbia Public Schools; and Anne C. White, Southwest Elementary.

Finally, we appreciate the support of our editor, Kelly Villella Canton, who guided us through the process and answered all of our many questions. We would also like to thank Karen Mason, Senior Production Project Manager at Pearson, and Susan McNally, Project Manager at Element LLC, for their work managing the production of this title.

The Importance of Engaging K–5 Students in Scientific Explanation

How can you support K–5 students in making sense of science ideas? How can you support students in constructing scientific explanations using evidence? Consider the following vignette from Mrs. Kyle's first-grade classroom.

Mrs. Kyle's first-grade class had been learning about magnets. The class wanted to find out the answer to the question, Are some magnets stronger than others? In an assessment of prior knowledge, many students indicated that they believed larger magnets were stronger than smaller ones. The students helped design three different tests about the strength of magnets. They used magnets of different sizes and shapes, and Mrs. Kyle intentionally

2

The
Importance
of Engaging
K–5 Students
in Scientific
Explanation

included a small, but very strong, bar magnet. The tests included investigating the number of paper clips each magnet could pick up (the clips were in plastic bags of 25), the number of chained paper clips that could be attached to a magnet, and the distance at which a magnet could attract a paper clip. After completing their tests of the different magnets and recording their observations, the first-graders gathered in a circle for a science talk to discuss their results.

> *Mrs. Kyle: What are the results of our tests to find out if some magnets are stronger than others?*
>
> *Sam: The bar magnet was the strongest.*
>
> *Mrs. Kyle: Were you surprised by that?*
>
> *Sam: Yeah, because it was the smallest.*
>
> *Mrs. Kyle: How do you know that the bar magnet was the strongest, Sam?*
>
> *Sam: The bar magnet could hold eight paper clips in a chain, the horseshoe magnet could only hold four paper clips, and the wand magnet could hold six paper clips.*
>
> *Mrs. Kyle: Did anyone else notice the same thing?*
>
> *Lauren: Yes, the bar magnet held the most in our group.*
>
> *Joe: That's not the same as our group.*
>
> *Mrs. Kyle: What did you find?*
>
> *Joe: We found that the bar and the wand magnet both held eight paper clips in a chain.*
>
> *Mrs. Kyle: What about the horseshoe magnet?*
>
> *Joe: It held four, so it wasn't that strong.*
>
> *Mrs. Kyle: What about the number of paper clips that were lifted? Did you find that the bar magnet was the strongest in that test?*
>
> *Olivia: Yes, the black bar magnet could lift the most, and then the wand, and then the horseshoe.*
>
> *Mrs. Kyle: Do other groups agree with Olivia's results?*
>
> *Several students: Yes!*
>
> *Mrs. Kyle: So what would you say about the magnets?*
>
> *Olivia: The bar magnet was the strongest.*

This vignette highlights important aspects of what it means to do science in elementary schools. Students worked to understand magnets and they were guided by a question about the strength of magnets. The teacher intentionally created a situation that challenged students' naïve ideas about larger magnets being stronger than smaller ones. Students designed and conducted tests to compare the strength of three magnets, and they recorded data/observations in their science notebooks (see Figure 1.1). Now students have come together as a group to share and discuss those observations. But what does it mean to engage students in scientific explanation? Let's extend the scenario and consider how the nature and purpose of the discussion changes from reporting results to constructing claims from evidence.

> Mrs. Kyle: Let's go back to our question: Are some magnets stronger than others? How would you answer that?
>
> Nate: Yes.
>
> Mrs. Kyle: Can you put your claim in a sentence, Nate?
>
> Nate: Some magnets are stronger than others.
>
> Mrs. Kyle writes the statement on a chart that has the question at the top: Are some magnets stronger than others? Beside the word claim she writes, "We found that some magnets are stronger than others."

FIGURE 1.1

Strength of Magnet Data Table

Magnet Type	1	2	3
	Number of paper clips lifted	Number of paper clips in chain	Distance magnet pulled a paper clip
Horseshoe 	25	4	3 cm
Bar 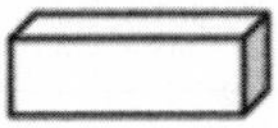	125	8	8 cm
Wand 	75	6	6 cm

4

The
Importance
of Engaging
K–5 Students
in Scientific
Explanation

Mrs. Kyle: What is your evidence for that, Nate?

Nate: Ummmm, the black magnet could lift more paper clips.

Mrs. Kyle: Can you look at your charts and give me some numbers to support Nate's claim?

Alison: Well, the black bar magnet lifted 125 paper clips, the wand magnet lifted 75, and the horseshoe only 25.

Mrs. Kyle: How does that go with our claim?

Alison: It tells us that the bar magnet is really strong and the horseshoe is not that strong.

Mrs. Kyle: And what does that mean?

Alison: It tells us that some magnets are stronger, like the bar magnet.

Mrs. Kyle: Should we include that as evidence for our claim?

Most of the class: Yes!

Mrs. Kyle writes on the chart: "Our evidence is that the bar magnet lifted 125 paper clips and the horseshoe magnet lifted 25, so the bar magnet is stronger than the horseshoe magnet."

Mrs. Kyle: Did we find the same evidence at our other stations?

Lauren: Yes, we found that the black bar magnet could hold more in a chain than the other magnets.

Joe: Except the wand magnet was the same for my group.

Mrs. Kyle: You're right, Joe. Can we still say that the bar magnet was stronger than the horseshoe with the evidence from your group?

Joe: Yeah, I guess—the bar magnet did hold more than the horseshoe.

Lauren: I think that we should write that about the bar magnet.

Alison: That would be more evidence.

Mrs. Kyle: I'm going to add that as more evidence. How many did the bar magnet hold in a chain?

Lauren: Eight, and the horseshoe held only four.

Mrs. Kyle adds to the chart: "We also found that the bar magnet could hold eight paper clips in a chain and the horseshoe could only hold four."

Mrs. Kyle: So we have written a claim to answer our question and we used evidence from our tests to support our claim. Who would like to read what we wrote for the class to hear?

Although sharing results is an important aspect of doing science, the second part of the vignette illustrates *moving beyond* results to constructing an explanation from evidence. More specifically, after results have been shared, the teacher guides students to propose a claim by returning to their original question about the strength of magnets. Students propose a claim—*Some magnets are stronger than others*—and consider their observations in light of that claim. In doing so, the class is able to support the claim by using multiple sources of evidence. How can you incorporate these kinds of scientific practices and talk with your students? This book will support you in exploring this question and provide you with research-based strategies for engaging K–5 students in constructing, communicating, and critiquing scientific explanations. In Chapter 1, we provide a rationale for engaging children with scientific explanation, share samples of written explanations, address the importance of intentionally connecting science and literacy, describe the benefits of engaging in scientific explanation for both students and teachers, and preview what to expect of students at different grade levels when it comes to scientific explanations.

Why Teach Children to Construct Scientific Explanations?

Fundamentally, science is about investigating and explaining how the world works. Scientists do not use a single "scientific method," but they do ask questions that frame their investigations of the natural world, have criteria for what data to collect and how to minimize human error, and rely on evidence derived from data to inform the development and critique of explanations. Similarly, young children are known to be naturally curious about how the world works. They explore enthusiastically, observe carefully, and ask important questions, such as *Why do some insects blend in with their environment but others have bright colors that get them noticed?* Until recently, the ability of children to engage in scientific practices and reasoning was underestimated, which in many cases translated to limited science learning opportunities in elementary school settings. Issues related to science in elementary grades are well documented and range from a lack of materials and high-quality curricula to an overwhelming emphasis on fun, hands-on activities that pay greater attention to "snacks and crafts" rather than big ideas in science. However, new research on young children's development provides compelling evidence that regardless of socioeconomic level, they come to school with rich knowledge of the natural world and the ability to engage capably in sophisticated reasoning and scientific thinking (Duschl, Schweingruber, & Shouse, 2007). But why focus on scientific explanations?

There are a number of important reasons for engaging elementary students in scientific explanation. Constructing and critiquing evidence-based explanations engages students in authentic scientific practices and discourse, which can contribute to the development of their problem-solving, reasoning, and communication skills. These abilities are consistent with those characterized as twenty-first century skills necessary for a wide range of current and future occupations

6

The
Importance
of Engaging
K–5 Students
in Scientific
Explanation

(Krajcik & Sutherland, 2009; National Academies, 2009). Constructing scientific explanations can also contribute to students' meaningful learning of science concepts *and* how science is done. Both components are necessary for scientific literacy and evidence-based decision making in a democratic society. As illustrated with the initial vignette, inquiry science is not only about collecting data and sharing results. By participating in the language of science, through talking and writing, students make sense of ideas and explain phenomena as they negotiate coherence among claims and evidence. This meaning-making process is essential to science learning and is supported through the construction of scientific explanations.

As mentioned previously, when science is actually taught in elementary school classrooms in the United States, the predominant approach has become hands-on activities, which can minimize the importance of big ideas and meaning making. There is much evidence to support this claim; however, the most striking may be the Trends in International Mathematics and Science Study (TIMSS) Video Study. This international comparison of science teaching at the eighth-grade level revealed that although U.S. lessons involved students in activities, the lessons placed little or no emphasis on the science concepts underlying those activities. More specifically, 44 percent of U.S. science lessons had weak or no connections among ideas and activities, and 27 percent did not address science concepts at all (Roth et al., 2006). In contrast, there were significant gains in science learning among students whose teachers were prepared to attend to a coherent science content storyline in their instruction. A coherent science content storyline focuses attention on how the ideas in a science lesson/unit are sequenced and connected to one another. Such storylines also concentrate on lesson activities to help students develop a "story" that makes sense to them (Roth et al., 2011). Our work with teachers in K–5 classrooms suggests that emphasis on scientific explanation and attention to developing a coherent content storyline are complementary efforts that can support student learning (Roth et al., 2009; Zembal-Saul, 2009). These ideas will be used later in the book to guide the planning process for science instruction.

Finally, in a recent synthesis of research from fields including science education and educational psychology, the National Research Council report, *Taking Science to School* (Duschl et al., 2007), and the companion document for practitioners, *Ready, Set, Science!* (Michaels, Shouse, & Schweingruber, 2008), make a strong case for the importance of science in elementary school classrooms. Those authors conceptualize proficiency in science around four interconnected strands (pp. 18–21).

- *Strand 1: Understanding Scientific Explanations* means knowing, using, and interpreting scientific explanations for how the natural world works. This requires that students understand science concepts and are able to apply them in novel situations, as opposed to memorizing facts.
- *Strand 2: Generating Scientific Evidence* requires knowledge and abilities to design fair tests; collect, organize, and analyze data; and interpret and evaluate

evidence for the ultimate purpose of developing and refining scientific models, arguments, and explanations.

- *Strand 3: Reflecting on Scientific Knowledge* involves understanding how scientific knowledge claims are constructed, both in scientific communities and the classroom. Students should recognize that scientific knowledge is a particular kind of knowledge that uses evidence to explain how the natural world works. They also should be able to monitor the development of their own thinking over time and in light of new evidence.
- *Strand 4: Participating Productively in Science* refers to norms of participation within the classroom community. For example, students should understand the role of evidence in presenting scientific arguments. The aim is to work together to share ideas, build explanations from evidence, and critique those explanations, much like scientists do.

An emphasis on evidence and explanation is not only overwhelmingly captured in the strands of science proficiency but it is also consistent with the framework for K–12 science education (National Research Council [NRC], 2011), national science education standards and reform documents (American Association for the Advancement of Science [AAAS], 2009, 1993, 1990; National Research Council [NRC], 2000, 1996). *A Framework for K–12 Science Education: Practices, Crosscutting Concepts, and Core Ideas* is one of the three fundamental dimensions of science education (NRC, 2011). (NRC, 2011) is engaging students in scientific practices, which includes constructing explanations from evidence and participating in argumentation. The *National Science Education Standards* (NRC, 1996) recognize the centrality of inquiry in science learning, emphasizing that students should "actively develop their understanding of science by combining scientific knowledge with reasoning and thinking skills" (p. 2). The content standards for abilities necessary to do scientific inquiry explicitly state that K–4 students should "use data to construct a reasonable explanation" and "communicate investigations and explanations." In addition, K–4 students should "think critically and logically to make the relationship between evidence and explanation" and "recognize and analyze alternative explanations." The *Benchmarks for Science Literacy* (AAAS, 2009) also include a similar focus on explanations and justifying claims.

The companion document to the *National Science Education Standards,* titled *Inquiry and the National Science Education Standards,* elaborates on inquiry as a content standard and describes five essential features of classroom inquiry that vary according to the amount of learner self-direction and direction from the teacher. These features include (1) learner engages in scientifically oriented questions, (2) learner gives priority to evidence in responding to questions, (3) learner formulates explanations from evidence, (4) learner connects explanations to scientific knowledge, and (5) learner communicates and justifies explanations (NRC, 2000, Table 2.6, p. 29). In this book, our approach to engaging students in scientific explanation addresses all four strands of proficiency, as well as the essential features of classroom inquiry, and will be illustrated through examples drawn from classroom science teaching.

Scientific Explanations in the Classroom

Our interest in students' construction of scientific explanations originated from research and professional development efforts with teachers participating in school–university partnerships and the education majors who interned in their classrooms. Two of the authors, Carla Zembal-Saul and Kimber Hershberger, first began their work specifically with elementary school science. The project was known as *TESSA: Teaching Elementary School Science as Argument* (Zembal-Saul, 2009, 2007, 2005) and the goal was to support teachers in scaffolding students in the process of using talk and writing tasks to negotiate the construction of evidence-based arguments in science. The use of the term *argument* in the TESSA project was based on the adaptation of Toulmin's Argument Pattern (Toulmin, 1958) and was intended to highlight the use of claims, evidence, and justification (the basic structure of an argument) in talking and learning science. Teachers and university faculty associated with TESSA worked to develop many of the strategies that are shared in this text. The other author of this book, Katherine (Kate) McNeill, and her colleague Joseph Krajcik began their work in a similar project with middle school teachers over ten years ago (McNeill & Krajcik, 2012). More recently, Kate has begun working with elementary school teachers on how to support younger students in scientific explanation in writing and talk (McNeill, in press; McNeill & Martin, 2011).

Both projects align with the framework for scientific explanation used in this book. In order to illustrate a scientific explanation, the following examples come from Kimber Hershberger's (third author) grade 3 classroom where students were investigating simple machines. Over the course of 6 weeks, the class tested levers, inclined planes, and pulleys to develop claims about the relationship among distance moved by the load and applied force. Students had used the structure of claims supported by evidence in prior science instruction.

In the first writing sample (Figure 1.2), Karen has drawn and labeled a representation of the class demonstration in which she, one of the smallest children in the class, was able to lift the teacher by using a lever. Below her drawing, she wrote a claim that responded to the question the class was investigating: "We can use a lever to lift teacher if we put the fulcrum closer to the load." Karen documented her observations, which she used as evidence to support her claim.

The second writing sample (Figure 1.3), also from Karen, is from a few weeks later in the unit on simple machines. For this investigation of inclined planes, the teacher designed a science notebook entry page that included the question, a data table for recording observations, and space for an explanation in which she prompted students to include claims, evidence, and scientific principles. Notice that Karen labeled the components of her explanation. It is evident in Karen's claim that she understood the relationship between reducing the force applied to lifting the load and increasing the distance of the inclined plane over which the force is applied to move the load. She wrote, "When you use inclined [plane] you use a greater

FIGURE 1.2

Karen's Explanation for How to Lift a Teacher by Using a Lever

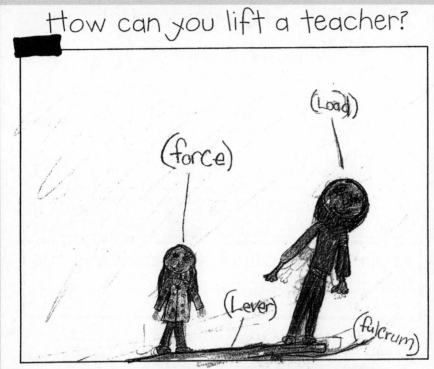

How can you lift a teacher?

(force)

(Load)

(Lever)

(fulcrum)

Explain what you learned about lifting heavy objects. (Use evidence from our experiments to support your ideas.)

We can use a lever to lift teacher if we put the fulcrum closer to the load. → When we used a bard (lever) and put a brick (fulcrum) close to the teacher (load) the student (force) was able to lift the teacher with a little effort.

distance but it takes less force to move the load." Karen also used data from her observations to compare the force needed for a straight lift (5N) to that needed to move the load to the same height using an inclined plane (3N); however, she did not include in her explanation the height to which the load was being moved (19 cm) or

10

The
Importance
of Engaging
K–5 Students
in Scientific
Explanation

FIGURE 1.3

Karen's Explanation for Inclined Planes

How do inclined planes help us to do work?

| How high are we lifting the load? 19cm 7in |
| How much force does it take to lift the load straight up? 500g 5 N |

	Distance of Board	Trial #1	Trial #2	Trial #3	Trial #4	Average
B	91 cm 36 in	200g 2N	200g 2N	200g 2N	200.5g 2.5N	200 g 2N
S	46 cm 18in	300g 3N	300g 3N	300g 3N	300g 3N	300g 3N

Explanation: (Claim, Evidence and Scientific Principles)

Inclined planes help us to move a load by reducing the effort or force we use but they increase the distance.

Claim: When you use inclined you use a greater distance but it takes less force to move the load.

Evidence: Our data shows that it takes 5 N to lift the load straight up and it takes 3 N of force to move the load using an inclined plane.

the distance across which the load was moved using the inclined planes (91 cm and 46 cm). She attempted to justify the connection between her claim and evidence by writing on a separate index card: "Inclined planes help us to do work by overcoming the force of gravity to move a load over a distance using less force." Although her justification was not robust, Karen did mention overcoming gravity (one of the scientific principles identified by the class).

Would it surprise you to know that Karen is a Title I student who struggled with academic writing? We selected samples of her work because they demonstrate the kinds of improvements that students are able to make in terms of writing explanations when norms of talking and writing scientifically are emphasized during science instruction. These changes can take place over short periods of time when consistently scaffolded by the teacher. For example, after discussing the components of scientific explanation as a class, Ms. Hershberger made a chart and hung it in the room for students to refer to during science talks and when writing explanations. She also emphasized the questions that students were attempting to answer through investigations by posting them in the room and including them on science notebook entry pages. These kinds of strategies are essential for supporting all students in constructing scientific explanation, especially younger students, students with linguistically diverse backgrounds, and students with special needs.

Throughout this book, we highlight strategies that can help different types of students successfully engage in constructing scientific explanations. Many of the strategies that work well for particular groups of students, such as English language learners (ELLs), are the same teaching strategies that work well for all students (Olson et al., 2009). The academic language of school science can be challenging even for native English speakers because of the specialized meanings of words (e.g., *matter, property, adapt,* etc.) and the unique features of science discourse (e.g., *the role of evidence*) (Gagnon & Abell, 2009). Consequently, we integrate our discussion of strategies for different learners throughout the book since they can be beneficial tools for all students.

Connecting Science and Literacy through Scientific Explanation

Since 2001 and the No Child Left Behind legislation, increased emphasis has been placed on helping *all* children develop literacy skills—reading, writing, speaking, and listening. In this political climate, science is not always seen as central to the education of elementary children, and often disappears from the school day to accommodate literacy instruction. However, a number of educators have argued that intentionally connecting science and literacy can enhance the learning of both (Hand, 2008; Hand & Keys, 1999). This may be something you are already attempting to do in your classroom. Inquiry-based science can provide a meaningful context for literacy activities in that it creates a motivating purpose for students to use language to negotiate meaning and figure out something new about the way the world works. Previous research suggests that inquiry-based instruction can successfully support ELLs in learning science content and language, particularly when

12

The
Importance
of Engaging
K–5 Students
in Scientific
Explanation

instruction takes into consideration students' cultural and linguistic backgrounds (Lee, 2005). In this book, our view of literacy is not confined to reading books about science content; rather, our focus is on talking, writing, and listening actively in science in ways that support negotiating and analyzing evidence-based claims.

Regardless of whether students are talking or writing explanations, language plays an essential role in learning science. When students are engaged in constructing, communicating, and critiquing science explanations, they make their thinking public (Bell & Linn, 2000; Michaels et al., 2008; Zembal-Saul, 2009). Talking about their thinking requires students to process their understandings as they attempt to articulate their ideas. Once that thinking has been made visible, peers can consider whether their understandings are consistent with or different from the ideas on the table, and they can ask clarifying questions. In addition to weighing one's ideas in light of those of others, making thinking visible also supports the establishment of social norms for talking and writing science in the classroom. For example, if a teacher consistently prompts for evidence to support claims, students in the class begin to recognize the need to use supporting evidence and to offer it without prompting. Another variation is that students start requesting evidence from one another to support claims. Finally, when science meaning is negotiated publicly, teachers can monitor both individual and group understanding. Put another way, constructing explanations from evidence provides the teacher with important assessment information about what students are understanding and how they are reasoning. In Chapter 4, we focus on establishing norms of participation in classrooms that engage students in constructing explanations from evidence, as well as the role of talk as a vehicle for teachers to monitor and assess student thinking and learning.

In our work in elementary classrooms, talking and writing science explanations are complementary activities. Sometimes we engage students in talking about their ideas first (e.g., predictions) in preparation for an investigation in which they will document observations in writing in their science notebooks, which will later serve as evidence for scientific claims. Other times we have students attempt to identify patterns in evidence and/or draft an initial claim in writing before gathering for a science talk in which we collectively construct claims from evidence. In order to monitor the thinking of the learning community over time and support the development of a coherent content storyline, we have developed scaffolds for talking and writing explanations, as well as strategies for mapping scientific explanations throughout a unit of study. These approaches will be shared in Chapters 4 and 5.

One approach to connecting the development of literacy skills and inquiry-based science instruction includes the use of science notebooks. There are a number of existing frameworks for science notebooks and writing in science, several of which we find particularly useful (Fulton & Campbell, 2003; Norton-Meier et al., 2008). In this text, we will describe our use of science notebooks in several chapters, placing specific emphasis on their role in engaging students with scientific explanations.

Benefits of Engaging Students
in Scientific Explanation

13

Benefits of
Engaging
Students in
Scientific
Explanation

As discussed previously, there are a number of important reasons to engage your students in scientific explanations that are consistent with contemporary thinking about science education in elementary grades and that attempt to improve scientific literacy. In addition, there are benefits to both students and teachers (McNeill, 2009; McNeill & Krajcik, 2008a; McNeill et al., 2006), which we will describe in more detail here. Benefits to students include understanding science concepts, participating in scientific practices, using evidence to communicate convincingly, and learning about the nature of science.

Understanding Science Concepts

When constructing evidence-based explanations, either through talking or writing, students use data/observations from their investigations and scientific ideas to answer questions about the physical world. This process can be seen as one of making sense of science concepts and applying them in flexible ways to new situations and is consistent with current perspectives on proficiency in science, particularly the strand that emphasizes knowing and using science explanations (Duschl et al., 2007; Michaels et al., 2008). Examining data for patterns and seeking coherence among claims and evidence are powerful thinking tasks that require students to reason scientifically. Such scientific reasoning can result in deeper understanding of science ideas as connections are made across the content storyline of a unit. For example, remember the earlier third-grade lessons on simple machines, when students made the connection between reducing the applied force and increasing the distance needed to move the load? Those children were observed relating that connection to simple machines studied later in the unit, such as inclined planes and pulleys. More specifically, the students not only recognized the connections but they also used the fact that the relationship held up in light of the other simple machines they studied. This suggests that those students were developing a meaningful understanding of the relationship and were able to apply that understanding in novel situations.

Participating in Scientific Practices

The ability to construct and communicate evidence-based explanations relies on being able to design and conduct fair tests and to collect, organize, analyze, and represent data appropriately—all essential scientific practices (Michaels et al., 2008). This kind of problem solving is essential to twenty-first century learning. Students can benefit greatly from reasoning logically about how best to collect data given the questions they have. For example, when kindergarten students recognize that during a seed investigation they need to change one variable (e.g., planting lima beans in dry soil versus wet soil), observe one key result (e.g., lima bean growth), and keep

14

The
Importance
of Engaging
K–5 Students
in Scientific
Explanation

everything else as similar as possible (e.g., amount of soil, placement in the classroom, etc.), they have developed the basis for thinking about fair tests. However, as illustrated through the opening vignette, this aspect of scientific practice must contribute to the ultimate aim of using those data to construct scientific explanations to the questions under investigation. Science lessons in K–5 often culminate with students sharing their observations. Unfortunately, lessons usually do not take that next step to include the construction of evidence-based explanations, which limits opportunities to engage students in this essential scientific practice.

Using Evidence to Communicate Convincingly

Science answers questions about the way the natural world works, and gives priority to the role of evidence in supporting scientific claims. When students communicate their thinking by proposing claims and supporting them with evidence, they benefit from participating productively in the norms of science and scientific language— strand 4 of science proficiency (Michaels et al., 2008). Moreover, students benefit by learning a powerful form of persuasive and empirical writing. Communicating in these kinds of complex ways also is central to twenty-first century learning and can be extended to other disciplines, as well as to students' everyday lives. For example, the importance of evidence in communicating convincingly in nonscience fields may take the form of determining which product to buy or deciding how to vote on a proposition that could affect local waterways. In real-world contexts, individuals need to be critical of the evidence and evaluate whether it is appropriate and sufficient for supporting particular claims. As it relates to school science and science learning, students not only benefit from constructing explanations but also from evaluating how peers are justifying claims and using evidence. Constructively critiquing the explanations of others involves active listening and clear communication. Teachers can effectively scaffold this kind of critical thinking and talk by asking students to agree or disagree with one another as they explain their evidence. As discussed earlier in association with making thinking visible, engaging in this kind of talk requires students to reflect on, organize, and articulate their thinking, which is a characteristic of strand 3 of science proficiency (Michaels et al., 2008).

Learning about the Nature of Science

Finally, by engaging in scientific explanation, students not only learn science concepts, but they also learn about the nature of science and scientific knowledge claims. Science is a social enterprise that involves large numbers of scientists working together. They discuss and debate their ideas at conferences and through publications, such as journals and books. For scientists, evidence plays a critical role in determining which ideas to support, modify, or reject. Because they are grounded in evidence, explanations can be tested by other scientists and are subject to change. When science is represented as a static body of facts, which is frequently the case in school curriculum, it fails to represent important aspects of science—that knowledge is created socially by scientists and changes in light of new tools, observations, and discoveries. Not only does it misrepresent science to portray it as a litany of known facts to be learned, but it also can discourage students from being interested in science. For these reasons, strand 3 of proficiency in science (Michaels et al., 2008), reflecting on scientific knowledge, specifically addresses the nature of science by having students recognize how their explanations change in light of new evidence, much in the same way scientists modify their explanations.

Our purpose in connecting benefits of engaging students in scientific explanation to the strands of proficiency in science is to illustrate how this approach to science teaching weaves the strands together in powerful ways. When emphasis is placed on evidence and explanation, children can develop meaningful understandings of science concepts, consider the important role of evidence in science, recognize science as a social endeavor through which explanations are changed in light of new evidence, and participate productively in a classroom community of scientists.

Benefits of Scientific Explanation for Teachers

Although understanding the benefits to students is important, it also is helpful to consider what teachers get out of learning to teach science in ways that engage students in scientific explanation. In our research with beginning elementary teachers, several benefits were observed when they adopted a stance to teaching science that gave priority to evidence and explanation (Avraamidou & Zembal-Saul, 2005; Zembal-Saul, 2009). First, when elementary teachers started to focus on scientific explanation, they also paid more attention to science content. This finding is not surprising, given that we define the science explanations that students construct as including important concepts in science. If a teacher is to intentionally facilitate students in constructing an explanation from evidence, it requires the teacher to have a deep understanding of that explanation and the investigations that generate the evidence necessary to support it. Because many elementary teachers are prepared as generalists, it is important to have access to reliable subject-matter resources when planning for instruction. In Chapter 3, we suggest a process that will help you recognize what you need to know about the science concepts, associated investigations, and children's ideas in order to effectively teach in this way.

Second, teachers who focused on scientific explanation also began to think about classroom talk and its role in learning differently (Zembal-Saul, 2009, 2007, 2005). Not only did these teachers come to recognize the importance of talk in making meaning of science ideas, but they also began to consider disagreement as potentially productive. Initially, many of the teachers we worked with shied away from "arguments" about claims and/or evidence. However, others observed that breakthroughs in learning often happened when students disagreed with one another. For example, a common source of disagreement stems from students conducting some

16

The
Importance
of Engaging
K–5 Students
in Scientific
Explanation

aspect of their testing differently across groups. Asking students to demonstrate their data-collection approach to the group and allowing for questions frequently result in students revising the test and/or coming to agreement about evidence. Negotiating effective science talks is potentially one of the most challenging practices for any teacher. In Chapter 4, we address scaffolds for classroom discourse, and in Chapter 5, we share instructional strategies that will help you be successful.

Finally, teachers in the research project who placed emphasis on evidence and explanation began to think about their role in working with small groups differently. When students are conducting investigations, it is common for teachers to visit each group, ask how students are doing, and assist with procedures. While the teachers in the project engaged in these kinds of supports, they also began listening for and documenting testable questions that emerged from the investigation and asking students about their data, the patterns they were noticing, and the kinds of initial claims they could draw from the data to respond to the question under investigation. These kinds of supports and questions are consistent with an emphasis on evidence and explanation, and they paralleled teachers' development in terms of increased attention to scientific explanation. In Chapter 4, we will provide question prompts for working with small groups during investigations. In addition, we will share strategies for organizing and representing data in ways that support young children in noticing relevant patterns in data that can form the basis of scientific claims.

What to Expect in Elementary Grades

Keep this important lesson in mind as you work to engage your students in scientific explanation. Although younger students are excellent thinkers and can readily begin to construct claims from their observations, as well as appropriately employ the language of evidence, it is not until students are older that they are ready to engage in some of the more complex aspects of this practice, such as applying scientific principles and suggesting and/or critiquing alternative explanations. As early as kindergarten, students can begin to use the term *evidence* when talking about their observations. For example, in a series of lessons about seeds and plants, kindergartners noticed that water was necessary for a seed to start growing. They observed seed changes in plastic bags with wet paper towels and in cups of damp soil. They also observed that seeds in dry soil did not change/grow. This collection of observations was used to create a claim about the role of water in seed development. Similarly, in the vignette at the beginning of the chapter, first-grade students used their observations of different kinds of magnets and the number of paper clips those magnets were able to pick up as evidence for their claim about the strength of magnets. The connection among question–claim–evidence is the most basic form of scientific explanation and is suitable for all grade levels.

As students tackle more substantial science content in grades 3 through 5, it is reasonable to consider having them use science principles to justify connections between claim and evidence, as well as consider alternative explanations. For example, in a fourth-grade lesson on adaptations, students noticed that although their hissing cockroaches shared common physical traits, they were still able to identify individual cockroaches within the group. The class constructed the claim: *Cockroaches in our group are similar, but not exactly the same.* Later, when introduced to the scientific concept that there is variation of traits in a population, students were able to use this idea to justify their claim in light of relevant evidence. As with justifying the relationship between claims and evidence, identifying and critiquing alternative explanations is more common among older students. However, this aspect of scientific explanation is quite sophisticated and not often observed in students' writing and talking.

At all grade levels, science notebooks are a useful way for students to document their tests, observations/data, and thinking over time. During science talks aimed at constructing explanations, we encourage students to bring their science notebooks with them and to refer to them during the discussion, especially when proposing evidence to support a claim. Even kindergarten children can develop meaningful notebook entries that use drawings and simple phrases to document their observations. Examples of K–5 student notebook entries will be included throughout the book.

As mentioned previously, we view talking and writing explanations as complementary activities. However, it is evident from our work with science explanations across the grade levels that co-constructing claims from evidence through science talks is an essential scaffold for learning, especially in the early grades. Norms for participating in the language of science should be made explicit to students and reinforced whenever possible. By actively listening to one another during science discussions, students develop an understanding of what counts as evidence and how to use that evidence to develop and support scientific claims. We often ask young students to record their observations and use them during science talks, but we rarely ask students to write scientific explanations before talking about their observations and identifying initial patterns in the data that serve as the basis for claims. As students become more familiar with developing science explanations and become more proficient writers, more responsibility for writing explanations individually can be transferred. The dynamic interplay between talking and writing scientific explanations is addressed throughout this book.

Check Point

In this chapter our goal was to introduce you to the potential of placing emphasis on scientific explanation in grades K–5. Samples of students' written work and examples of science talks were used to illustrate how engaging in scientific explanation can help all children learn science concepts and participate in the language of science. We demonstrated how scientific explanation is aligned with national standards and reform documents in science education. More importantly, we

18

The
Importance
of Engaging
K–5 Students
in Scientific
Explanation

showed how engaging in this significant practice contributes to students' meaning making and literacy development, including students with culturally and linguistically diverse backgrounds and special needs. In addition, we provided some initial insights regarding what to expect at various grade levels. At this point, we hope you are curious about the framework and how to use it in your classroom. In subsequent chapters, we will describe the framework for scientific explanation in detail and provide examples of students' explanations across grade levels and content areas, share strategies for generating evidence and for supporting students in talking and writing explanations, and propose approaches for planning instruction and assessing student work. Taken as a whole, this book is intended to help you effectively engage all students in the complex scientific practice of explanation building.

Study Group Questions

1. Discuss the similarities and differences between science lessons that are merely *hands-on* and those that engage students in scientific explanation.
2. After reading this book and trying some of the approaches with your students, you become interested in developing a greater emphasis on scientific explanation in your science teaching. How will you justify your decision to your principal? Craft a convincing argument to recruit one of your colleagues to try it with you.
3. It has been suggested that connecting literacy activities to inquiry-based science instruction can enhance the learning of both by creating a meaningful and motivating context. Describe at least one way you can create this kind of connection with your students.
4. Before moving on to the chapter describing the framework for scientific explanation, what questions do you have about teaching with an emphasis on scientific explanations? About how engaging students in scientific explanation supports their meaningful learning? About assessing students' explanations? Others?

A Framework for Explanation-Driven Science

How can you support the development of scientific explanations in your teaching? What does a scientific explanation look like in science talks and in science writing? Consider the following vignette from Ms. Marcus's second-grade classroom.

Ms. Marcus was starting a unit on light and asked her class to look for shadows in the classroom. The students were surprised that they could find shadows in the room and even more surprised when they realized that when they pulled the blinds, the lights in the room still made shadows. They wanted to know if other sources of light would make shadows. With the help of their teacher, the students set up light stations to see if they could make shadows with a variety of sources of light, including a black light, a flash-light, a candle, a desk lamp, and a television. After investigating the shadows of different light sources, the class gathered in a circle for a science talk.

Ms. Marcus: What did you observe as you went around to our light stations?

Paul: All of the lights made shadows!

Ms. Marcus: Did that surprise you?

Paul: Yeah, I really didn't think that the candle would make a shadow.

Ms. Marcus: What did you notice about the shadow at the candle station?

Jamie: The candle made the best shadow.

Ms. Marcus: Do other people agree with Jamie?

Lisa: Yeah, but really they all made pretty good shadows.

Ms. Marcus (pointing to a sentence strip): Our question was "Can we make shadows with any kind of light source?" How can we answer that question?

Alex: Any kind of light will make a shadow.

Ms. Marcus: Do you think we can make that claim from our investigations?

Mark: Well, not really since we didn't test __all__ kinds of lights.

Alex: But, if we did I think they would make a shadow.

Mark: You're probably right but since we didn't check, I think we should say: Light from different sources makes shadows.

Ms. Marcus: So is that the claim should we write on our KLEW chart?[1]

Most students give the sign for yes.

Ms. Marcus: What is our evidence?

Lisa: We tested different kinds of lights and they all made shadows.

Mark: I think we should say which lights we tested.

Ms. Marcus: How would you like to write it?

Mark: We tested a black light, flashlight, desk lamp, candle, and TV, and they all made shadows.

Jamie: On the white paper.

---

[1]KLEW is a modification of the reading comprehension strategy, KWL. The acronym allows us to map the following ideas over time: what students think they *know* about a science question or topic (K), what they are *learning* stated as claims (L), what *evidence* they are using to support each claim (E), and what new questions or *wonderings* they have (W). We have found that these charts can serve as an important scaffold for supporting students in scientific explanations. We will discuss them in more detail in Chapter 5.

Ms. Marcus (writes): Light from different sources makes shadows. Our evidence is that we tested a black light, a flashlight, a candle, a desk light, and a TV, and we saw that they all made shadows on the white paper.

Maria: We should add because light travels in a straight line.

Ms. Marcus: How do we know that?

Lisa: We tested it with red Jello™ and a laser light, and we saw the light going in a straight line.

Ms. Marcus: Why is that important?

Maria: Cause that's why we get shadows.

Ms. Marcus: Can you say more about that?

Maria: The light travels in a straight line until something blocks it and that makes a shadow.

Ms. Marcus: That's our scientific reasoning. I'm writing: We saw the shadows because the light was traveling in a straight line until our objects blocked it. Is that okay?

Maria: Yeah, good.

In this vignette, the second-grade class was negotiating an explanation for the question, *Can we make shadows with any kind of light source?* The students discussed their ideas about which light sources make shadows and backed up those claims using evidence from their investigations. Ms. Marcus used questions and other strategies to support her students in engaging in this complex scientific talk.

How can you help your students participate in scientific explanations? In this chapter, we discuss a framework (i.e., claim, evidence, reasoning, and rebuttal) to support students in explanation-driven science in both talking and writing. Throughout the chapter we revisit the vignette from Ms. Marcus's classroom to illustrate the different components of the framework. We also use a video clip from a third-grade classroom to demonstrate how to introduce the framework to your students, and writing samples from students in a variety of content areas and grade levels to illustrate how to apply the framework. Furthermore, we describe variations of the framework that increase in complexity that you can use with your students, depending on their prior experiences with this important scientific inquiry practice, and we discuss benefits of the framework for all learners.

Framework for Explanation-Driven Science

Engaging in scientific inquiry can be challenging for students, in part because they are not familiar with the norms in science. Science is a way of knowing with particular ways of thinking, reasoning, talking, and writing (Michaels et al., 2008).

A key aspect of science is the role of building and debating explanations. To support students in this complex practice, we have adapted Toulmin's model of argumentation (1958) in order to develop a framework for scientific explanation (McNeill & Krajcik, 2012; McNeill et al., 2006; Zembal-Saul, 2009) that consists of four components: *claim*, *evidence*, *reasoning,* and *rebuttal*. With elementary students, we typically focus on either the first two components (claim and evidence) or first three components (claim, evidence, and reasoning) of the framework, particularly in terms of students' writing. Rebuttals are often not introduced until middle school or even high school. Yet, in this section, we describe all four components to provide an overview of the entire framework. We begin this important scientific inquiry practice by describing the first two components, claim and evidence, and how they can be used to support early elementary students as well as students with little prior experience in explanation. Figure 2.1 illustrates these first two components.

Claim

The first component of the framework is the *claim*. The claim is the statement or conclusion that answers the original question or problem. Creating a claim that specifically answers the question can be quite challenging for elementary students. Often, students will provide an answer that addresses the topic (e.g., states of matter), but does not directly answer the question (e.g., Is rice a solid, liquid, or gas?). Consequently, it can be important to support students in constructing claims that specifically address the question being asked. Furthermore, students' claims can address the question, but initially be either too specific or too general considering the data available to the students. Crafting an appropriate claim can take revision and practice as a whole class.

For example, in the opening vignette, Ms. Marcus asked her students to consider their observations across the various stations in order to develop a claim that responds

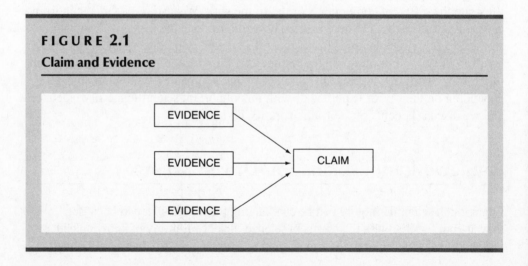

FIGURE 2.1
Claim and Evidence

to the question, *Can you make shadows with any kind of light source?* During the discussion, one student proposed a claim, but then another student refined the claim to make it more accurate. More specifically, the initial claim was: *Any kind of light makes a shadow.* However, because the class did not test all possible light sources the claim became: *Light from different sources makes shadows.* The final version of the claim still addressed the question and was more accurate given the available evidence. Furthermore, because the claim was negotiated publicly during the science talk, all members of the class had access to the thinking behind the revision process, which can be particularly beneficial for English language learners. This enabled all the students to develop a stronger understanding of what counts as an appropriate claim.

Evidence

An essential component of science is the use of *evidence.* When scientists construct or revise claims, they do so using evidence. Consequently, we want even young students to be using evidence to support the claims that they make in science. Evidence is scientific data that support the claim. Data are observations or measurements about the natural world. Data can be qualitative, such as the colors of plants, or they can be quantitative, such as the heights of plants. Both quantitative and qualitative data play important roles in science; however, students can have a more difficult time seeing qualitative data as evidence. Initially, it can be easier for students to recognize "numbers" as evidence. Thus, it is essential to help students develop an understanding of what does and does not count as evidence.

As students develop an initial understanding of evidence, we can also introduce the ideas of *appropriateness* and *sufficiency* of data (although not necessarily using those terms). Data are *appropriate* for a claim if they are relevant or important to answer the specific question or problem. For example, students may use inappropriate data, like their everyday experiences, as evidence for the claims they make in science. In fact, this is quite common among younger students. Although it is important to connect to students' everyday experiences and we want to help students see that science is all around them in the world, it is also important to help students develop an understanding of scientific evidence. More specifically, evidence in science comes from observations and investigations about the natural world. You have a *sufficient* amount of data if you have enough to support your claim. In science we often use multiple pieces of data as evidence to support our claim. For example, Figure 2.1 illustrates that there are three pieces of evidence supporting the claim. Initially, when you introduce the framework to your students, you might want to focus on only one piece of evidence, but as the children gain more experience and expertise you should encourage them to use multiple pieces of evidence to support their claim. The specific number of pieces of evidence will depend on the particular learning task or investigation that students complete. There is not an ideal number of pieces of evidence (i.e., three pieces); rather, students should be using all appropriate evidence that is available to make their claim.

In the vignette, we saw Ms. Marcus's students using multiple pieces of qualitative data to support their claim. After the class refined their claim and recorded it, Ms. Marcus specifically asked her students, *What is our evidence?* As with the claim, the students' first attempt to articulate evidence was vague: *We tested different kinds of lights and they all made shadows.* Suggestions from other students involved adding the specific light sources tested and information about shadows being made on a white paper surface. Consequently, as a class, the students refined their evidence to include qualitative data (i.e., they made shadows) from five different investigations: *Our evidence is that we tested a black light, a flashlight, a candle, a desk light, and a TV, and we saw that they all made shadows on the white paper.* In this case, the evidence that was included was relatively brief yet still included five different pieces of evidence.

Reasoning

After students become comfortable using evidence to support their claims, you can then introduce the third component of the framework: *reasoning*. Reasoning is a justification that connects the evidence to the claim. The reasoning shows why the data count as evidence by using appropriate and sufficient scientific principles. Figure 2.2 expands the initial framework to add the reasoning component that is explaining that link between the claim and evidence.

Articulating their reasoning is a more complex process for students. For elementary students, we have found that reasoning is more challenging than the claim and evidence components (McNeill, 2011). This also is the case for older students in middle school (McNeill & Krajcik, 2007; McNeill et al., 2006) and

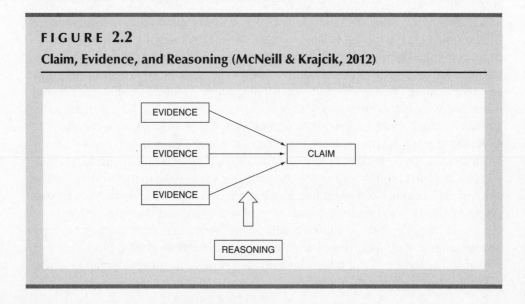

FIGURE 2.2
Claim, Evidence, and Reasoning (McNeill & Krajcik, 2012)

in high school (McNeill & Pimentel, 2010). Students can have a difficult time explaining how they used scientific principles or scientific ideas to decide what counts as evidence. Instead of explaining how or why the evidence supports their claim, students' initial reasoning sometimes ends up being just a repetition of their claim and evidence. Instead, the reasoning should include the big science idea or science concept that is the focus of the lesson. Including the reasoning encourages students to consider and reflect on these science ideas, as well as provides them with the opportunity to become more comfortable using scientific terms and language.

For example, in the opening vignette, the class ends up including the following statement as their reasoning: *We saw the shadows because the light was traveling in a straight line until our objects blocked it.* Prior to this investigation, the second-grade class had completed several investigations that allowed them to observe that light travels in straight lines until it is blocked by an object, which makes a shadow. This scientific principle allowed students to justify the connection between the claim and evidence, which we refer to as *reasoning.* Including the reasoning encourages students to use the big ideas in science to articulate how or why evidence supports their claim.

Rebuttal

Finally, the last component in the framework is the *rebuttal.* The rebuttal recognizes and describes alternative explanations and provides counterevidence and counter-reasoning for why the alternative explanation is not appropriate. Figure 2.3 adds the rebuttal to the scientific explanation framework.

FIGURE 2.3

Claim, Evidence, Reasoning, and Rebuttal (McNeill & Krajcik, 2012)

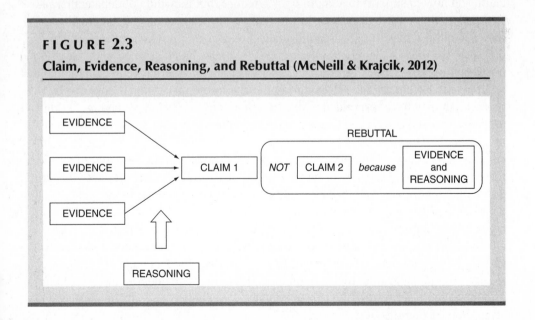

Often, scientists debate multiple alternative claims and try to determine which claim is more appropriate. As Figure 2.3 illustrates, the rebuttal explains why an alternative claim (Claim 2) is not a more appropriate claim for a specific question. Similar to the original claim (Claim 1), the rebuttal uses both evidence and reasoning. But in the case of the rebuttal, the evidence and reasoning articulate why Claim 2 is not appropriate.

Rebuttals are another challenging aspect of scientific explanations. In our work with elementary students, we have not explicitly named or discussed this component of the framework. Rather, as our examples will illustrate, the teachers we have worked with have chosen either to focus just on claim and evidence, or on claim, evidence, and reasoning. Particularly in terms of students' writing, this is not something we typically see until middle school or high school. Yet, in looking at students' science talk, we often see students debating multiple claims, which engages students in the process of a rebuttal even if we do not specifically name it as such. For example, in discussing what plants need to grow, one student may make the claim that plants do not need soil to grow (Claim 1), whereas another student may claim that plants do need soil to grow (Claim 2). The discussion and investigations that then occur in the classroom will allow the students to collect data and make sense of those data to determine which of the two claims is more appropriate. Engaging in this process includes the use of rebuttals, which is an important component of science, but explicitly naming that process as rebuttal may not be productive for elementary students. In contrast, we find that using the language of claim, evidence, and reasoning can help support students in understanding the practice of science and the expectations around how to support and justify a claim in science.

In Ms. Marcus's lesson, the class discussed how to refine the language of their claim and how to support that claim with evidence, but they did not debate alternative explanations. We feel that the level of talk in the vignette is quite sophisticated (but also quite achievable) for second-grade students, and it was not necessary to introduce the idea of the rebuttal. However, if students had disagreed with Alex's initial claim—*Any kind of light will make a shadow*—an alternative explanation and rebuttal may have naturally arisen during the classroom discussion. For example, one student may have responded with a common misconception by saying, "I don't think all light sources make shadows because the moon is a light source, but everything is dark at night so the moon does not make shadows." If this alternative claim had arisen that only some light sources make shadows, additional evidence and reasoning would have needed to be considered to determine which of the two claims was more appropriate. The teacher could then ask students to go outside at night when the moon is out to collect data about whether the moon creates shadows or she could go out at night and take photos that she would bring in as additional data to discuss as a class. In this case, multiple explanations would have been considered, and yet we still feel that it is not necessary to introduce the language of "rebuttal" to second-graders. Rather, focusing on the ideas of claim, evidence, and reasoning provides a more simplified and easier framework to engage students in constructing scientific explanations.

At this point we thought it might be helpful to use a video example to illustrate how you can introduce the framework to your students. Video 2.1 is from Ms. Hershberger's third-grade class from 2009–2010. Students have been investigating inclined planes as part of a unit on simple machines. Although the class has some prior experience using the language of claims and evidence, Ms. Hershberger reviews the components of scientific explanation with students and supports them in constructing working definitions for each component. She then creates a poster using students' language for explanation, which is displayed in the classroom for the rest of the year and used by the class as a reference when talking and writing scientific explanations.

VIDEO 2.1

Introducing the CER Framework

In the discussion prior to this video clip, students were identifying patterns in data for force and distance that they had collected during an investigation in which they were trying to answer the question, *How do inclined planes help us do work?* Ms. Hershberger wants the class to write a scientific explanation associated with their investigation, so before they begin the writing task, she prompts them to reconsider the parts of an explanation. She chooses to emphasize the first three components of the framework: claim, evidence, and reasoning. Watch the 6-minute video clip from this lesson. Ms. Hershberger uses a variety of strategies during the discussion of the framework to help students develop a better understanding of claim, evidence, and reasoning, and to link this framework to their prior experiences. These strategies and others will be described in more detail in Chapter 5.

The clip begins with Ms. Hershberger asking the class about the three parts of a scientific explanation. After the students identify claim, evidence, and scientific principles from their prior science learning experiences, Ms. Hershberger asks more specifically, "What is a claim?" Not surprising, given the earlier part of the discussion about inclined planes, students respond with claims specific to the current investigation. She prompts students to think more generally about how claims are made and what is useful in crafting a claim. When the class continues to focus on the specific investigation and data that students collected for inclined planes, she asks, "How do we begin an investigation?" This question helps shift students' thinking to focus on the question as the driving force behind an investigation. After students revisit their question for the inclined plane investigations, they are much better able to describe the claim as a statement that answers the question. Ms. Hershberger writes this definition on chart paper using students' words. Her approach of eliciting students' ideas and connecting the definition for *claim* to the current investigation stands in contrast to providing the class with a standard definition. Ms. Hershberger's approach is student-centered and encourages ownership of the framework among students.

In the next part of the science talk Ms. Hershberger asks, "You have the claim, but what else do you need?" The students immediately make the connection that claims are based on evidence from the inclined plane investigation. Nevertheless, the teacher pushes further by asking, "Where does evidence come from?" The class describes the evidence for a claim coming from their investigation data, and one student adds, "If you didn't have data, how would you even answer the question?" In this way, students are able to relate data and evidence back to the claim. One child elaborates on this to explain that if you have data that do not support the claim, then you may need to consider a different claim. Although rebuttal is not addressed specifically in the discussion of scientific explanation, this point suggests that at least some members of the class are considering the important need for "fit" between data and claim, and the need to consider alternative explanations when the fit is not complete. Once again, Ms. Hershberger records the definition for evidence on chart paper using students' language for reference in future investigations and explanation development.

When Ms. Hershberger asks the class about reasoning as a component of explanation in the next part of the discussion, they already know that it requires the use of scientific principles. For this unit, Ms. Hershberger kept a running record of "big ideas" in science intended to help students think about their investigations. More specifically, the list of scientific principles for simple machines included ideas such as work, force, and friction. Through the discussion, students come to describe the role of scientific principles as helping with the "why" for a claim–evidence connection. One student adds that scientific principles help to tell the "whole story" of the explanation. Because they had been referring to principles in prior instruction, Ms. Hershberger introduces *reasoning* as a component of explanation, but still uses students' words to create the definition.

The claim, evidence, reasoning framework is a lot for K–5 students to process at one time. Ms. Hershberger's approach of engaging students in science investigations in which they became familiar with drawing conclusions from data allowed her to introduce claim, evidence, and reasoning as components of scientific explanation much more easily and to attach these components to students' prior experiences. By recording the definitions for the components of explanation in students' own words and posting them in the classroom, Ms. Hershberger and her class have a meaningful tool that they will use again and again during the school year as they engage in science writing and discussion.

The scientific explanation framework can be used across the different content areas in science—life science, earth and space science, and physical science. In this section, we provide a specific example from each content area to further illustrate the framework, as well as discuss other topics to which the framework can be applied.

Life Science Example

In life science, there are many topics where students can either collect or be given data to analyze. The scientific explanation framework can support students' meaning making, either in talk or in writing, as they try to make sense of the data and develop a stronger understanding of the science concepts. For example, the framework can be applied when investigating topics such as the needs of plants, the needs of animals, adaptations, behaviors, life cycles, inherited and acquired characteristics, similarities and variation among organisms, food webs, habitats, senses, the human body, nutrition, and germs. All of these topics provide opportunities in which students can either collect data or they can be asked to make sense of data that have been given to them.

For example, one third-grade teacher we worked with was teaching a unit on plant growth. He had his students plant seeds and place one pot with seeds in direct sunlight, while the other pot with seeds received no direct sunlight. Over two weeks, the students collected observational data of the leaves, stems, roots, and flowers, as well as quantitative data about the height of the plants, which they recorded in their science notebooks. After collecting all of their data, the teacher asked the class to construct a scientific explanation that answers the question, *Do bush bean plants grow better in direct sunlight?* The teacher was looking for his students to write scientific explanations similar to the claim, evidence, and reasoning shown in Table 2.1. He did not ask his students to include a rebuttal, but we included the rebuttal in the table to illustrate what it might look like. He wanted students to make a claim: *Bush bean plants grow better in direct sunlight.* Next, he wanted them to include at least three pieces of evidence such as the plant heights, the number of leaves, and the color. Finally, the reasoning provides a justification that links the claim and evidence. In this case, the reasoning is fairly simple: *Height, number of leaves, and color are all important for a plant's health. Since the plant in direct light was taller, had more leaves, and was dark green, that means it was able to grow better.* Figure 2.4 shares a sample of writing from one of the third-grade students in the teacher's classroom.

In order to provide the student with feedback, the teacher underlined the claim, numbered the evidence, and circled the reasoning in addition to his written comments. In this example, we see the student provided the appropriate claim: *Bush beans gro[w]*

TABLE 2.1 Examples of the Different Components of Scientific Explanations

Question	Claim	Evidence	Reasoning	Rebuttal
Life Science Do bush bean plants grow better in direct sunlight?	Bush bean plants grow better in direct sunlight.	The plant in direct sunlight grew 16 cm, and the plant with less sunlight grew 11 cm. The plant in direct sunlight had 6 leaves, and the plant with less sunlight only had 3 leaves. Finally, the plant in direct sunlight was a dark green, and the plant with less sunlight was pale green.	Height, number of leaves, and color are all important indicators of a plant's health. Since the plant in direct light was taller, had more leaves, and was dark green, that means it was able to grow better.	On day 2, the plants looked the same, so you might think that light does not matter. But after 2 weeks, the height, leaves, and color were different.
Earth and Space Science How can sun shadows be used to tell time?	The length of the sun shadow can be used to tell time.	At 10:45 a.m., the shadow was 20 cm and the sun was low. At 12:25 p.m., the shadow was 17 cm and the sun was high. Finally, at 2:15 p.m., the shadow was 21 cm and the sun was low. Shadows are longer in the morning and afternoon, and they are shorter at noon.	The length of the shadow is determined by how high the sun is in the sky. The sun changes position in the sky because the earth rotates once each day. When the sun is higher in the sky, the shadows are shorter, which is why they can be used to tell time.	Someone may think that shadows cannot be used to tell time because they have nothing to do with the time of the day. Someone may just think shadows are determined by the object that makes the shadow. But the shadow for the same object actually changes over the course of the day.
Physical Science Does the number of turns of the rubber band affect the distance the vehicle travels?	The number of turns does affect the distance a vehicle travels.	When we turned the rubber band 4 times it traveled 45 cm, and when we turned it 8 times it traveled 63 cm.	Turning the rubber band transforms kinetic energy into stored or potential energy. The stored energy then transforms into kinetic energy when the rubber band is released. Kinetic energy is energy of movement. The more times the rubber band is turned, the more stored energy there will be upon transformation, which means the more kinetic energy there is. That is why the more you turn it, the farther the vehicle travels.	Some people may think that the number of times the rubber band is turned does not affect the distance because they do not realize that the rubber band stores energy and that is why the vehicle moves. They may think it moves just because it has wheels or because someone can push it. But the energy comes from the wound rubber band.

FIGURE 2.4

Third Grade Scientific Explanation about Bush Bean Plants

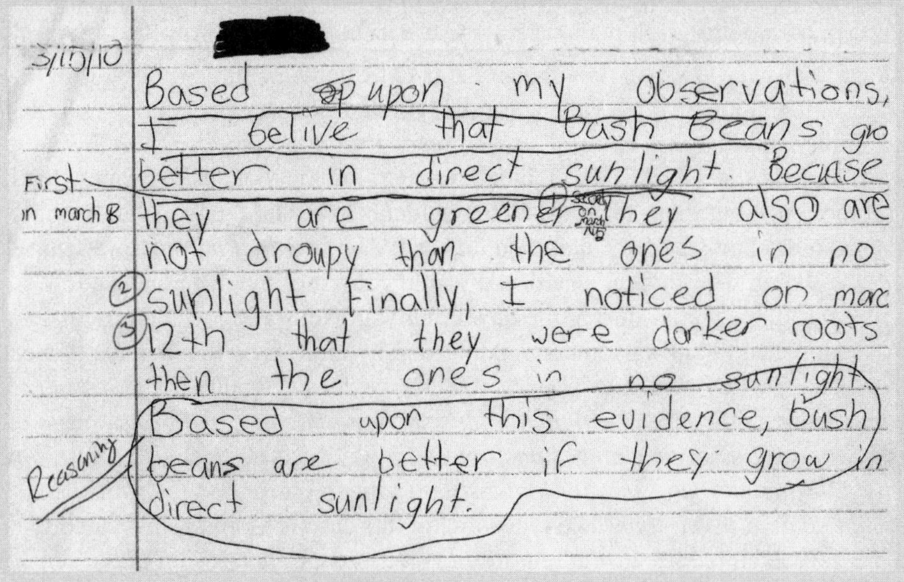

better in direct sunlight. The student then included three pieces of evidence: *Because on March 8 they are greener. Second on March 12 They also are not droopy than the ones in no sunlight. Finally, I noticed on Marc[h] 12th that they were darker roots then [sic] the ones in no sunlight.* The student also provided some initial reasoning linking the evidence to the claim: *Based upon this evidence, bush beans are better if they grow in direct sunlight.* Neither the evidence nor reasoning is as detailed as the ideal example in Table 2.1. In particular, the reasoning just illustrates restating the evidence and claim, rather than describing how or why the evidence supports the claim. Yet, the student is successfully justifying her claim with some evidence and reasoning. Although she has room to improve, this student is having some success using the framework to help her both make sense of her data and to engage in science writing.

Earth Science Example

There are many opportunities in earth science to construct scientific explanations. Students can analyze data either from their own investigations or data that have been given to them for topics such as weather, properties of soil, rocks and minerals, fossils, erosion, weathering, earthquakes, volcanoes, the water cycle, seasons, phases of the moon, position of the sun, and shadows. All of these topics provide multiple opportunities to support students in constructing scientific explanations in talking and writing.

For example, one fifth-grade teacher asked her students to write a scientific explanation that addressed the question, *How can sun shadows be used to tell time?* In order to answer this question, the students collected data three times during the day (morning, noon, and afternoon) for the length of the shadows in their schoolyard. Table 2.1 illustrates an ideal student response for this question. Similar to the last example in life science, we included a rebuttal in the table to illustrate what it might look like, but the teacher asked her students to include only a claim, evidence, and reasoning. The student's claim would state: *The length of the shadow can be used to tell time.* The student's evidence would consist of the different shadow lengths at different times during the day. Finally, the reasoning would articulate why shadow length allows someone to tell time by discussing the idea that the earth rotates once per day, which is why the sun changes position in the sky. Specifically, the reasoning might state: *The length of the shadow is determined by how high the sun is in the sky. The sun changes position in the sky because the earth rotates once each day. When the sun is higher in the sky, the shadows are shorter, which is why they can be used to tell time.* The reasoning in this case is more sophisticated than the previous example because it requires a more in-depth discussion of the scientific principles in order to articulate why the evidence supports the claim.

Figure 2.5 includes the scientific explanation from one of the fifth-grade students. He provided a correct and accurate claim: *Sun shadows could be used to tell time by the length [sic].* Interestingly, the next section that the student labeled as evidence included some of his evidence in terms of describing the general trends, such as *in the morning when the sun is low the shadows are long.* The rest of his evidence is actually at the bottom of the page where the student provided the specific times and specific lengths of the shadows. Across the two sections, the student's evidence is accurate and complete, although the different locations bring into question whether the student understood that the specific numbers should be included as part of his evidence. Finally, the reasoning started to explain why the evidence supports the claim in that it states: *Sun shadows can tell time because the earth moves, so time changes.* The student made a link between the movement of the earth and the length of the shadows, but this movement of the earth was not described in depth nor did the student discuss how this affects the position of the sun. This example illustrates how the framework is helping to support the student in writing his scientific explanation, yet his reasoning could be more in depth.

Physical Science Example

The physical sciences provide students with multiple opportunities to analyze data. There are numerous investigations students can conduct in class to collect their

FIGURE 2.5

Fifth Grade Scientific Explanation about Sun Shadows and Time

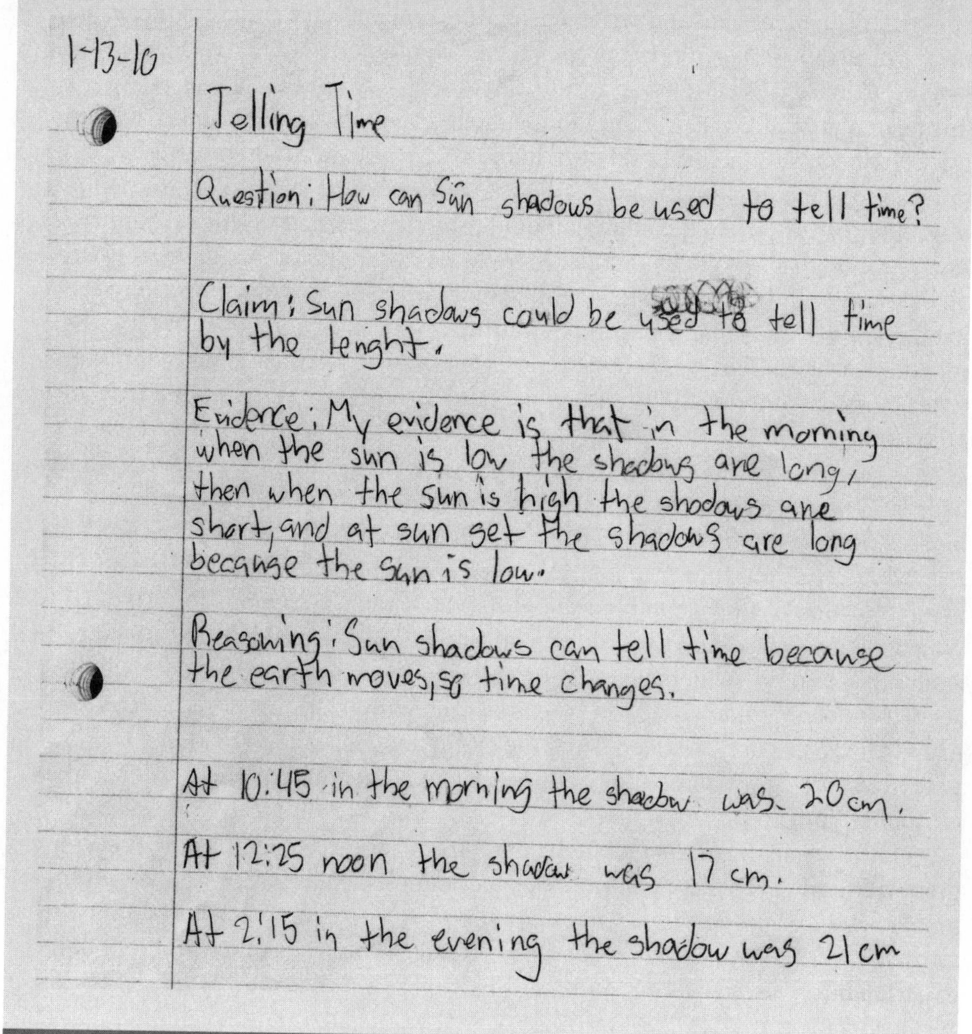

1-13-10

Telling Time

Question: How can Sun shadows be used to tell time?

Claim: Sun shadows could be used to tell time by the lenght.

Evidence: My evidence is that in the morning when the sun is low the shadows are long, then when the sun is high the shadows are short, and at sun set the shadows are long because the sun is low.

Reasoning: Sun shadows can tell time because the earth moves, so time changes.

At 10:45 in the morning the shadow was 20cm.

At 12:25 noon the shadow was 17 cm.

At 2:15 in the evening the shadow was 21cm

own data, or they can analyze data that are provided to them. For example, data can be analyzed around topics such as properties of objects, properties of substances, substances interacting with each other, states of matter, changes in states of matter, force, motion, energy, light, heat, electricity, magnetism, and sound. Students can then construct explanations in which they justify their claim with appropriate evidence and reasoning.

For example, a fourth-grade teacher was completing a unit with her students on the topic of force, motion, and energy. The students were testing rubber band cars in which the rubber band was wound around the axle. When the rubber band unwound it caused the axle to spin and move the car. Specifically, she had her students collect data and write a scientific explanation to address the question, *Does the number of turns of the rubber band affect the distance the vehicle travels?* Table 2.1 illustrates an ideal student response for this question. Again, this example includes the rebuttal in the table, even though the teacher did not ask her students to include a rebuttal in their writing. The student would analyze the data to come up with this claim: *The number of turns does affect the distance a vehicle travels.* Then the student would provide specific evidence from the investigation that illustrates that the more turns of the rubber band, the further the vehicle traveled. Finally, the reasoning would articulate why turning the rubber band results in the vehicle traveling a farther distance. Specifically, in the reasoning, the teacher is looking for the students to discuss potential and kinetic energy, which they had previously discussed in class: *Turning the rubber band transforms kinetic energy of the winding into stored or potential energy. The stored energy is then transformed into kinetic energy when the rubber band is released. Kinetic energy is energy of movement. The more times the rubber band is turned, the more stored energy there is, which means the more kinetic energy there is. That is why the more you turn it, the farther the vehicle travels.* This example requires the application of fairly complex scientific ideas in the reasoning. If the students were younger or had less experience with scientific explanations, we would expect a simpler reasoning statement, such as the light example in the vignette with the second-graders or the bush bean plant example with the third-graders. In this example, the teacher had been using the claim, evidence, and reasoning framework with her students for some time and she expected them to include fairly complex reasoning in their writing.

Figure 2.6 includes a specific example from another student in the fourth-grade classroom. This student provided a complete and accurate claim—*Yes the number of turns on the rubber band around the axel effects [sic] the distance of the vehicle.* The student then went on to provide two pieces of evidence from her experiment: *When we wind it 8 times, it moved 63 cm. When we wind it 4 times, it moved 54 cm.*

Finally, the student provided sophisticated reasoning in which she discussed both stored energy and kinetic energy: *My reason is that when we wind it it is called stored energy, but when we release it it is called kinetic energy. Stored energy means that it is ready to be released and move. Kinetic energy is when you release the stored energy. The more you wind it, the more energy ready to be released and move the vehicle.* Although there are some grammatical errors in the writing, the student clearly explained her ideas about why winding the rubber band impacts the distance traveled by the vehicle and incorporated the scientific ideas of stored energy and kinetic energy into her writing.

FIGURE 2.6

Fourth Grade Scientific Explanation about Energy

Does the number of turns effect the the distance the vehicle travels?

Yes the number of turns on the rubber band arround the axel effects the distance of the vehicle. First we connected the rubber band to the vehicle. Then we turned the axel that spins. And when we let it go, it moved. When we wind it 8 times, it moved 63 cm. When we wind it 4 times, it moved 54 cm. My reason is that when we wind it. It is called stored energy, but when we release it it is called kinetic energy. Stored energy means that it is ready to be released and move. Kinetic energy is when you release the stored energy. The more you wind it, the more energy ready to be released and move the vehicle. When you wind it a little bit, of energy, it some energy will be ready. When you have alot, more will be ready.

The complexity of the claim, evidence, and reasoning will depend on how you design the learning task as well as the age and experience of your students. In this section, we purposefully selected writing samples from third-, fourth-, and fifth-grade students because all of the examples include some reasoning. We wanted to illustrate what the different components could look like across different science content areas. In discussions (such as the second-grade vignette), we also see younger students articulating their reasoning at times. Yet, typically in K–2 classrooms, students' writing focuses on just the claim and evidence components of the framework. Throughout the book, we will include other examples from these earlier grade levels. Here we included more sophisticated examples to illustrate what the components can look like when students gain more experience using the framework in both science talks and science writing.

Increasing the Complexity of the Framework over Time

There are multiple variations of the scientific explanation framework that you can use with your students, depending on their level of experience and comfort level with this type of science talk and science writing. Table 2.2 provides a summary of these different variations of the framework. Variations 1–3 are typically used in elementary classrooms, whereas Variation 4 is more likely to be used in middle school or high school classrooms. This final variation (Variation 4) can also be broken down into greater complexity for more experienced students, which we describe in other work (see McNeill & Krajcik, 2012).

In this section, we describe and provide an example to illustrate Variations 1–4. The example throughout focuses on the same overarching science concept that objects can be described by both the materials of which they are made and their properties. Two objects made of different materials (or different substances) have different physical properties. For instance, a metal spoon and a plastic spoon both have the same use (e.g., eating), but they have different properties (e.g., color, hardness, flexibility, solubility) because they are made of different materials. Although all four examples focus on this key science concept, the complexity of the science content and the complexity of the scientific explanation increases across the four variations.

Variation 1: Claim and Evidence

Variation 1 of the framework focuses on simple patterns in data that allow for a claim to be generated and supported with one piece of evidence. We have found that this variation of the framework works well with kindergartners and first-graders, and that it is an appropriate starting place for even older students if they have minimal experience with this scientific inquiry practice. This initial framework focuses on constructing a claim that specifically answers the question asked, rather than a statement about the general topic that does not address the question. Furthermore, Variation 1 targets providing one piece of evidence that supports the claim. This includes the idea of *appropriate* evidence, although we would not recommend using that term with inexperienced students. Rather, students should focus on whether the evidence answers the question being asked and supports the claim.

For example, kindergarten students can investigate the science concept that objects can be described in terms of both the materials of which they are made and their physical properties. Their teacher provides them with a variety of objects (e.g., spoons, balls, and blocks) and asks them to sort the objects based on the material of the object (i.e., what the object is made of). Specifically, they are asked to answer this question: *Which objects are made of different materials?* After sorting the objects, the class comes together for a science talk in which they

TABLE 2.2 Variations of the Instructional Framework for Scientific Explanation

Level of Complexity	Framework Sequence	Description of Framework for Students
Simple	*Variation 1* 1. Claim 2. Evidence	*Claim* • A statement that answers the question *Evidence* • Scientific data that support the claim
	Variation 2 1. Claim 2. Evidence • Multiple pieces	*Claim* • A statement that answers the question *Evidence* • Scientific data that support the claim • Includes multiple pieces of data
	Variation 3 1. Claim 2. Evidence • Multiple pieces 3. Reasoning	*Claim* • A statement that answers the question *Evidence* • Scientific data that support the claim • Includes multiple pieces of data *Reasoning* • A justification for why the evidence supports the claim using scientific principles
Complex	*Variation 4* 1. Claim 2. Evidence • Multiple pieces 3. Reasoning 4. Rebuttal	*Claim* • A statement that answers the question *Evidence* • Scientific data that support the claim • Includes multiple pieces of data *Reasoning* • A justification for why the evidence supports the claim using scientific principles *Rebuttal* • Describes alternative explanations, and provides counterevidence and counterreasoning for why the alternative explanation is not appropriate

discuss their results. A student could potentially offer the following scientific explanation:

> *The two spoons are different materials (Claim), because one is white and the other is silver (Evidence).*

In this example, the student provides a claim that specifically answers the question being asked and she uses one piece of evidence from her investigation (i.e., the color of the two spoons). Using the evidence in this case is really important because it provides a rationale for why she decided the two spoons are different materials. Initially, students may just provide their claim and you will need to encourage them to use evidence (i.e., their observations and measurements) to explain why they came up with that claim. Most claims in science are better supported by multiple pieces of evidence. But if your students are new to thinking about the idea of using evidence to support a claim, it can help students initially to focus on one piece of evidence.

Variation 2: Using Multiple Pieces of Evidence

Variation 2 includes a focus on multiple pieces of evidence. As students gain more experience with this complex practice, students can construct explanations with a claim supported by more than one piece of evidence. More experienced or older children can debate about the strength of the evidence that they use to support their claim. The idea of using multiple pieces of evidence aligns with the concept of including *sufficient* evidence, although, once again, we do not necessarily recommend using that term with elementary students. Rather, we would talk about including *multiple* pieces of evidence or considering whether or not we have *enough* evidence to support our claim. Including multiple pieces of evidence also provides the opportunity to use and discuss different types of evidence, such as both quantitative and qualitative data. This can encourage students to think about what does and does not count as evidence in science.

Returning to the previous example in which the students were sorting the different objects, this investigation can also be used for Variation 2 of the framework. The students are still addressing the question, *Which objects are made of different materials?*, but now they need to include multiple pieces of evidence to support their claim. For example, one potential student explanation could be:

> *The two spoons are different materials (Claim). My evidence is that one spoon is white and the other spoon is silver (Evidence 1). The white spoon is also softer, because I can scratch it with my fingernail while the silver spoon is harder because I cannot scratch it (Evidence 2). Also, the two spoons are the same size, but they weigh different amounts. The white spoon was 3.0 grams and the silver spoon was 16.4 grams (Evidence 3).*

In this example, the student is making the same claim as in Variation 1, but in this case there are three pieces of evidence to support the claim. One student may come up with all three pieces of evidence. Yet another possibility is that during a science talk focused on the class results, various students generate the different pieces of evidence and the teacher records the multiple pieces of evidence on the board or on another visual so that the students can observe all the evidence that they came up with as a class. The example also includes both qualitative evidence (e.g., color and hardness) as well as quantitative data (e.g., the mass of two objects

39

Increasing
the
Complexity
of the
Framework
over Time

that are the same size).[2] This can provide an interesting opportunity to discuss what observations and measurements the students can use as evidence to address their overarching question of which objects are made of different materials.

Variation 3: Providing Reasoning

As students become more comfortable supporting claims with evidence, reasoning can also be introduced to students as a more complex variation of this practice. In the reasoning component, students need to explain why their evidence supports their claim. The reasoning includes the scientific principles or big ideas in science and articulates how the students are using these ideas to make sense of their data. Articulating this link between the claim and evidence can be challenging for students, because they need to describe how or why their evidence supports their claim. Initially, when using the framework it may be more appropriate to focus only on the claim and the evidence. As students gain more experience and comfort, the reasoning component can be added to the framework. In some of the classrooms in which we have worked, students as young as second and third grade have successfully begun to include the reasoning in both their science talk and writing. We have also worked with teachers who have decided to wait until fourth or fifth grade to introduce reasoning, mainly because they felt their students first needed more experience with using evidence to support their claims.

For the example about the properties of materials, the reasoning can be added onto the previous scientific explanation in order to articulate how or why the evidence supports the claim. For example, a student could create the following scientific explanation:

> *The two spoons are different materials (Claim). My evidence is that one spoon is white and the other spoon is silver (Evidence 1). The white spoon is also softer, because I can scratch it with my fingernail while the silver spoon is harder because I cannot scratch it (Evidence 2). Also, the two spoons are the same size, but they weigh different amounts. The white spoon was 3.0 grams and the silver spoon was 16.4 grams (Evidence 3). Color, hardness, and mass for the same size of objects are properties of materials. If two objects have different properties, they are different materials. Since the two spoons have different properties, I know they are different materials (Reasoning).*

---

[2]The mass of two objects of the same size is focusing on the idea of *density* even though it does not use this term. Density can be a challenging concept for students, so you may or may not want to discuss this idea with your students. *Mass* by itself is not a property that allows you to determine if two objects are made of the same material (or substance). For example, you can have 8 ounces of water or 32 ounces of water. In both cases, they are water, but the mass will be different. On the other hand, if you have 8 ounces of water and 8 ounces of oil, the mass will be different because they are different substances that have different densities.

This example is identical to the previous one in terms of the claim and evidence. The one addition is that in the reasoning, the student describes why the evidence supports the claim. Specifically, the explanation includes the main science concept that different materials have different properties, which is why the two spoons can be separated or grouped as different materials. Including the reasoning encourages students to really think about the key science concept and how to articulate that science concept in either talk or writing.

Variation 4: Including a Rebuttal

The last variation includes the addition of the rebuttal. A rebuttal describes alternative explanations and provides counterevidence and counterreasoning for why the alternative is not appropriate. As we mentioned previously, the rebuttal is the most complex component of the framework, and it may not be appropriate to refer to this component by name with elementary students. As students continue on to middle school and high school, it becomes more important to encourage students to incorporate this alternative perspective in their writing. Yet the idea of a rebuttal may very well emerge during science talks, particularly if there is disagreement around a particular claim. If multiple potential claims emerge, the class will want to discuss the strength of those claims and what evidence and reasoning the class has to support the claims.

This last example is from an older and more experienced classroom (e.g., fifth grade). Consequently, in addition to adding the rebuttal, this example also uses more scientific or academic language. In the *National Science Educations Standards* (NRC, 1996), there is a shift in the language of the standards from K–4 to 5–8 in which discussion focuses on properties of *substances* instead of properties of *materials*. A substance is something that is made of the same type of material (atom or molecule) throughout. And so, in this example the students are answering the question, *Which objects are made of different substances?* In discussing whether the two spoons are made of the same substance, a potential student misconception is that "use" is an important property to identify whether two objects are made of the same substance. Some students in the class may provide this claim: *The white and silver spoon are the same substance (Claim) because they are both used for eating (Evidence).* As the two different claims are discussed (the two spoons are the same versus different substances), rebuttals will emerge as part of the classroom discussion. Consequently, the following scientific explanation could be constructed as a class:

> The two spoons are different substances (Claim). My evidence is that one spoon is white and the other spoon is silver (Evidence 1). The white spoon is also softer, because I can scratch it with my fingernail while the silver spoon is harder because I cannot scratch it (Evidence 2). Also, the two spoons are the same size, but they weigh different amounts. The white spoon was 3.0 grams and the silver spoon was 16.4 grams (Evidence 3). Color, hardness, and mass for the same size of objects are properties of

substances. If two objects have different properties, they are different substances. Since the two spoons have different properties, I know they are different substances (Reasoning). Some people may think the two spoons are made of the same substance, because they are both used for eating. But use is not a property that tells us what an object is made of. Use cannot tell you if two objects are made of the same substance (Rebuttal).

This scientific explanation includes similar claim, evidence, and reasoning as Variation 3 with the use of the term *substance* instead of *material.* The one major addition is the rebuttal, which makes the scientific explanation itself more complex in terms of the structure; furthermore, the science content is more complex because it specifically addresses the idea of whether or not use is a property. Although you may not want to have students include the rebuttal in their writing, multiple potential claims may arise in your classroom. An important aspect of science is that scientists debate the appropriateness of different claims as well as the strength of the evidence and reasoning to support those claims.

We present the four different variations to illustrate there are multiple ways to engage your students in scientific explanations. You should select the variation that is most appropriate for your students, considering their previous experiences and age. You also may decide that over the course of the school year you might want to shift from one variation to the next as your students gain more experience with this scientific inquiry practice. For example, you could introduce the framework in terms of Variation 1 at the beginning of the year and add on the idea of multiple pieces of evidence as your students become more comfortable. Alternatively, with more experienced students you may want to begin with Variation 2 and then add the reasoning component as your students become better able to express their evidence to support their claims. The framework should be adapted to meet the specific needs of your students.

Benefits of the Framework for All Learners

Elementary classrooms consist of an academically diverse group of students, including students with special needs and English language learners. Meeting the needs of all learners is a challenging task. Yet, the strategies discussed throughout this book will help all students achieve greater science proficiency. Using an integrated approach to teaching science and literacy can support ELLs in learning both science and language. It also can support native speakers of English in developing a deeper understanding of the complex language of science (Pray & Monhardt, 2009). Teachers need strategies to help build both the language and content knowledge of all of their students in order for students to succeed in science (Olson et al., 2009). Using the claim, evidence, and reasoning framework can be an essential tool to support teachers in this task.

Science includes specialized ways of communicating, which can differ from students' everyday ways of talking and writing. Students from culturally and linguistically diverse backgrounds can prioritize forms of communication, such as storytelling (Bransford, Brown, & Cocking, 2000), different from the forms prioritized in science. In order to help all students learn science, it is important to develop an understanding of students' everyday ways of knowing and to make the implicit rules of science discourse explicit (Michaels et al., 2008). Elementary students can understand terms such as *evidence* and *explanation* from their everyday lives, which can be resources for science instruction. For example, we conducted a study in a diverse urban elementary school where we asked fifth-grade students at the beginning of the year what they thought it meant to "use evidence" and to "create an explanation" in their everyday lives as well as in their science class (McNeill, in press). When speaking about using evidence in their everyday lives, the majority of students talked about an exchange between people, such as when a person wants to convince someone, but they were less likely to talk about evidence as data or that one uses evidence to support an idea or claim. For explanation in their everyday lives, they also talked about an exchange between people, such as when someone explains why a person was out in a baseball game. When asked about creating an explanation in science class, the majority of the students said they did not know what it meant. Over the course of the school year, their teacher, Mr. Cardone, made connections to their everyday understandings and used the claim, evidence, and reasoning framework to support the students in developing stronger understandings of these ideas in science class as well as stronger science writing.

Consequently, it can be important to understand your students' everyday meanings and ways of knowing as well as discuss how these are similar and different from scientific ways of knowing. The students' understandings can vary, depending on their cultural and linguistic backgrounds. The scientific explanation framework can also serve as a tool to help students understand your expectations for what it means to justify a claim in either talk or writing in science class. The framework simplifies this complex scientific inquiry practice into components, which may be more accessible to students. Explicitly discussing the framework for science talk and writing may encourage more students to participate and successfully engage in the discourse in your classroom.

The different variations of the framework also serve as a resource to better support all students. The backgrounds, experiences, and understandings of your students will influence which variation of the framework is appropriate for your classroom. Furthermore, you can use the different variations in order to differentiate instruction to meet the needs of particular students. Differentiating instruction includes individualizing lessons to meet the needs of each student in an academically diverse classroom (Adams & Pierce, 2003). For example, one teacher we worked with focused her instruction on Variation 3 in that she required all of her students to justify their claims with appropriate evidence and reasoning. However, as a class, they also talked about the concept of a rebuttal, as when you disagree with another individual's claim. When some of her more advanced students completed their writing early, she challenged them to add a rebuttal to their writing. Consequently, the different variations of the framework can be used to individualize instruction to meet the specific needs of your students.

Check Point

At this point, we have discussed why scientific explanation is important to integrate into your classroom practice. We have also described a framework (i.e., claim, evidence, reasoning, and rebuttal) that you can use to support all students in scientific explanations. Furthermore, we have illustrated what introducing the framework can look like in a third-grade classroom, provided examples of scientific explanations across various content areas, and described different variations of the framework that can be adapted to meet the needs of your students. In the upcoming chapters, we will focus on how to get the evidence you need for scientific explanations. In order to create scientific explanations successfully, students need to have data to analyze, so this is a key aspect of the practice. Furthermore, we will discuss different teaching strategies you can incorporate into your instruction as well as how to plan for integrating explanations in your classroom. Finally, we will focus on assessment, providing strategies for designing assessments and rubrics as well as examples of how the assessments can be used to evaluate the strengths and weaknesses of your students to better meet their needs in your instruction.

Study Group Questions

1. Select a science concept that you currently teach your students. What is a question you could ask your students to create a scientific explanation? Write out a sample potential student explanation labeling the claim, evidence, and reasoning (and rebuttal if you would like) for that question.
2. Examine Table 2.2. What variation of the framework will you introduce to your students? Why do you feel that variation is appropriate?
3. How will you introduce the framework to your students? How will you define the different components?
4. Introduce the scientific explanation framework to your students. What worked well? What challenges arose? How would you introduce it differently in the future?

3

Planning For Explanation-Driven Science

How can you design instruction that provides your students with opportunities to construct scientific explanations? How can you identify opportunities in your current curriculum where your students can construct scientific explanations? What kinds of supports can you provide students for successfully engaging in this complex practice? Consider the following vignette of Miss Carpenter and Dr. Zeeland preparing for a kindergarten unit on seeds and plant growth.

> Miss Carpenter is a mentor teacher in a local school–university partnership. She was preparing to teach a unit on seeds and plants, and invited Dr. Zeeland, the university science education liaison, to join her. They began by examining a variety of documents, including the district curriculum concepts and outcomes for the unit, the state and national science standards, and a variety of trade books related to the unit topic. The unit concepts were

(1) there are many kinds of plants; (2) plants have roots, stems, and leaves; and (3) different kinds of plants grow from different seeds. Miss Carpenter noted that these concepts were related to national life science standards for K–4, specifically life cycles and characteristics of organisms: (1) plants and animals have life cycles; (2) plants require air, water, nutrients, and light; and (3) plants and animals have different structures that serve different functions (NRC, 1996, p. 129). Dr. Zeeland added that the inquiry standards also were relevant—asking questions about organisms/objects in the environment, planning and conducting a simple investigation, employing simple tools to gather data, using data to construct a reasonable explanation, and communicating investigations and explanations (NRC, 1996, p. 122).

Both educators were part of a professional learning community that was considering how to frame instruction around a coherent science content storyline. The notion of a storyline involves establishing and maintaining learning goals, linking ideas and activities within and across lessons, and sequencing ideas and activities in logical ways that allow students to follow the storyline and construct meaning (Roth et al., 2011). Miss Carpenter and Dr. Zeeland designed a planning matrix to help them focus on the components of explanation, as well as the development of a coherent storyline (Table 3.1). First, they identified the key concepts of the unit and sequenced them in a meaningful way based on what they knew about children's prior knowledge of seeds and plants. The key concepts were added to the chart in the form of claims that kindergarten children were capable of making. Because the role of claims in a science explanation is to respond to questions about phenomena, Miss Carpenter and Dr. Zeeland turned their attention to crafting appropriate questions to guide instruction. Next, they considered what kinds of observations would be necessary to serve as evidence from which the claims could be generated. Finally, the specific activities and investigations from which evidence could be collected were added to the chart.

At the end of this process, Miss Carpenter noted that the content storyline and explanation building opportunities did not follow the sequence of the unit concepts as portrayed in the curriculum guide. She and Dr. Zeeland decided that this was defensible, given that all key concepts and learning goals were met, and that the re-sequencing allowed for more connections to be made across concepts. Miss Carpenter also remarked how different the process was from her usual approach, which involved collecting and reviewing activities that matched unit topics. In her work with Dr. Zeeland, the activities were actually the final consideration in the planning sequence.

Because her students were not experienced with constructing science explanations, Miss Carpenter developed a mystery bag activity to introduce questions, claims, and evidence (see Norton-Meier et al., 2008). This activity

TABLE 3.1 Science Content Storyline for Kindergarten Seed Lessons

Questions	Claims	Evidence	Activity
Questions should be testable in some way. Students should know what the question is that they are trying to answer through their investigations.	A claim is a statement based on evidence that answers the question. *These statements should reflect unit science concepts and/or student learning outcomes.*	Evidence is a pattern in observations/data from which the claim is generated.	Activities should be carefully selected to provide the appropriate opportunities for observations/data collection necessary for evidence.
What is a seed?	[Some] plants grow from seeds.	Lima beans (seeds) grow into a plant. [1–3] Other kinds of seeds grow into plants. [4] When we open the wet/swollen lima beans, we can see the baby plant (embryo), plant food, and root (radical). [2]	**1. Lima Bean Activity A** Explore children's prior knowledge about seeds. Have students observe dry lima beans and record observation in their journals. Do they think it is a seed? What do they think it needs to start growing?
What do seeds need to start growing? *Add something about what they need to keep growing later.*	Seeds need water/moisture to begin growing. Seeds do not need soil to grow at first. Seeds contain everything necessary to start growing a plant.	Lima beans start to *change* (swell, seed coat splits) and grow when they get wet. [2–3] The lima beans in the baggies with a moist paper towel grow. The lima beans in the moist soil grow. [3] A variety of seeds grow when they get moist. [4] A variety of seeds in the baggies with a moist paper towel grow. [4]	**2. Lima Bean Activity B** *Accidentally* get the lima beans wet. Have students observe again and record changes from their initial observations. Open the seeds and notice what is inside. Record in journals.
What are the parts of a plant and how do they grow?	Plants have stems, roots, and leaves. Many plants have a similar pattern of growth.	*Use drawings/photos of observations as evidence. Be sure to label drawings.* [1–4] Observations should show that the root usually grows first, then the stem, and then the leaves.	**3. Lima Bean Activity C** Place seeds in baggies with damp paper towels and observe/record over time. *One variation is to place some seeds in soil and some in baggies and compare.*
Are all seeds alike?	Seeds come in a variety of shapes, sizes, textures, and colors. Some seeds sprout faster than others.	For each of the following there should be observations about physical characteristics (shapes, sizes, colors, textures) and germination time. Lima beans [1–3] All of the other seeds students tested [4] *A chart would be a good way to represent these data.*	**4. Seed Variety Activity** Present students with a variety of small objects and ask which ones are seeds. Have them think back to lima bean activity to figure out what will allow them to figure it out (adding water). Set up the test and record predictions about which will grow. Document observations.
What is a plant?	Plants are living things.	*Use observations about how plants grow and change to support this claim. Create opportunities for students to observe what happens when plants get too much or too little water, too little sunlight, etc.*	
Are all plants alike?	There are many different kinds of plants. Most plants share a variety of features in common.	*Use drawings of observations here.* [5] [4] Most plants are green. Most plants have leaves, roots, and stems.	**5. Plant Variety Activity** Note that different seeds grow into different plants. [4] Bring in a wide variety of plants. Ask students to classify them as plants or not using evidence—green, leaves, stems, roots. Also have them draw/note differences in the shape of the leaves, etc.

*requires students to make observations of an object concealed in a paper bag
using three "tests" (e.g., pick-up, shake and listen, touch but not look), and
to construct a claim about what is in the bag based on these observations.
In addition, Miss Carpenter prepared a large chart on which students could
record their daily observations with drawings and photographs, and a bul-
letin board on which to post claims that the class constructed from evidence.
She also prepared several science notebook pages for children to use to
document their thinking throughout the unit.*

This scenario illustrates how a kindergarten teacher and her colleague prepared a
unit that addresses important science content, creates a coherent storyline, and is structured in a way to provide opportunities for children to pursue interesting questions,
make and document observations, and construct claims based on evidence. In planning the unit, they considered both the relevant science content and inquiry standards.
They also attended to supports that children might need to engage in the construction
of science explanations. By using the planning matrix (Table 3.1), Miss Carpenter and
Dr. Zeeland were able to keep the focus on science ideas and explanation rather than
falling into the trap of planning a unit around a collection of fun activities.

In this chapter, we examine how you can plan for instruction that purposefully
integrates opportunities for all students to engage in constructing scientific explanations. We address how you can use the components of a coherent science content
storyline to inform your instructional planning. In addition, we introduce data and
scientific principles as the essential features of scientific explanation, as well as how
to attend to them as part of your planning. Finally, we discuss how you can vary the
complexity of the learning tasks you develop to better support your students in constructing explanations. Examples of learning performances from a variety of grade
levels and content areas are provided, and specific attention is given to how to adapt
existing curriculum materials to support scientific explanation.

Coherent Science Content Storyline

As mentioned in Chapter 1, one of the concerns about science instruction in elementary schools is that the approach has overwhelmingly been one of hands-on
activities. Certainly, active engagement on the part of learners is desirable, but the
results of the TIMSS Video Study, a comparison of teaching across five countries,
reported that in the United States these activities typically placed little emphasis on
the underlying science ideas or, worse yet, were not connected to science concepts
at all (Roth et al., 2006). In other words, students were provided with directions and
required to complete activities without having to think about the science or engage
in reasoning. The notion of a coherent content storyline was developed from observations of science teaching in high-achieving countries in which science ideas were
central to instruction, and hands-on activities were intentionally linked to concepts

and to one another. Constructing scientific explanations requires that students use big ideas in science to make sense of data. Because developing a coherent storyline requires a focus on the central ideas in science, going through this process can help you develop a science curriculum that provides multiple opportunities for students to develop scientific explanations.

So what does it mean to create a coherent content storyline? The fundamental notion of storyline is to create a "big picture" by purposefully selecting and sequencing science ideas in ways that build on one another. The following teaching strategies can be useful in creating a content storyline (Roth et al., 2011).

- *One main learning goal:* The learning goal is a complete science idea, not a topic or phrase. For example, "Seeds" is a topic. A related learning goal might be "A seed is the part of a plant that contains the baby plant (embryo) with its protective coat and stored food that can develop into a new growing plant under proper conditions."

- *Goal statements and/or focus questions:* The goal statement or focus question should be aligned with the learning goal and phrased appropriately using language that students can understand. Ideally, students should not know the answer to the question at the beginning of the lesson. An effective focus question can be used throughout the lesson to elicit prior knowledge, guide investigations, and inform the development of claim statements. Recall that claims are constructed to answer the focus question, so a well-phrased question is essential to constructing scientific explanations.

- *Activities match the learning goal:* Activities/investigations should provide opportunities for students to interact with and observe phenomena related to the learning goal. Whenever possible, investigations should allow for students to collect data that can be used as evidence in constructing the scientific explanation. Activities/investigations should be intentionally selected to contribute to students' developing understanding of the learning goal.

- *Content representations match the learning goal:* As students construct explanations from evidence, they will eventually need to be introduced to scientific principles that will allow them to reason about the connection between claims and evidence. Content representations, such as analogies, diagrams, and models can serve to illustrate principles. Representations should make sense to young learners, be scientifically accurate, and match the learning goal.

- *Content ideas linked to other content ideas:* Explicit connections among science ideas *across* lessons support the development of deep understanding and are central to the notion of a coherent content storyline. This may involve linking to previous or subsequent lessons, or connecting to an overarching question. This form of linking is essential to constructing compelling scientific explanations.

- *Key ideas and activities sequenced appropriately:* For much science content, the order in which ideas are introduced can influence the ability to make connections and build deeper understanding. Sequencing ideas and activities appropriately requires a great deal of thought and careful planning. Keep in mind that the goal is to create a coherent storyline that builds to a big-picture explanation.

- *Synthesis of key ideas:* At the end of a lesson or lesson sequence, ideas need to be tied together. Having students discuss or write their scientific explanation—including claims, evidence, and reasoning—is an effective synthesis approach.

In our work with preservice and practicing teachers, we have found that using coherent content storylines to frame planning can be a powerful tool. Moreover, studies examining this approach demonstrate significant gains in science learning among students whose teachers were prepared to attend to a coherent content storyline in their instruction (Roth et al., 2011). Developing a coherent storyline can help all students learn science, including students with special needs. In describing teaching strategies that support science success for students with special needs, Steele (2007) argues for the importance of creating science lessons based on big ideas. Focusing on a few important ideas helps students with special needs pay attention to the key ideas and not get lost in numerous details. Furthermore, developing a storyline can support all students in making connections across lessons and in building stronger understandings over time.

Essential Features for Constructing Scientific Explanations

Although planning instruction around a coherent content storyline is fundamental to effective science teaching, it does not ensure that students will have opportunities to construct scientific explanations. We see constructing scientific explanations and developing a coherent content storyline as complementary activities. Our research suggests that when teachers adopt a focus on evidence and explanation in their science teaching, they also attend more closely to science content (Zembal-Saul, 2009, 2007, 2005). It stands to reason that these approaches work well together given that scientific explanations are by their very nature *about* science ideas. The teacher must consider what those ideas are in order to create opportunities for students to pursue testable questions, collect and analyze appropriate data, and construct and justify claims from evidence. Consider Miss Carpenter in the opening vignette. Her planning with Dr. Zeeland began with identifying the main science ideas and learning goals for the unit and stating them as claims that kindergarten children are capable of constructing. It was only in the final phases of planning that they selected specific activities intended to provide the necessary evidence for building claims.

As you consider the science talk and writing in your classroom, you will find there are times when one of the main learning goals is to have students construct a claim and support it with evidence and reasoning. However, you will encounter important science learning tasks for which the framework for scientific explanation does not align. For example, you may want your students to (1) define the term *seed* and (2) provide several examples of plants that grow from seeds. Both of these tasks can be effective questions for assessing children's understanding. Responses to the first question provide you with a sense of whether students can define a seed as the part of a plant that contains the baby plant (embryo) with its protective coat and stored food that can develop into a new plant under proper conditions. The second part can help you assess whether students are aware of the kinds of plants that grow from seeds (e.g., flowering plants, trees, grass). The goals of these questions are different from asking students to construct a scientific explanation in which they would apply their understanding of seeds to make sense of data and construct a claim from evidence. It is important to consider learning goals when planning opportunities for constructing scientific explanations. You will need to think about what it is you want children to *do* with their knowledge of the science ideas and if that goal aligns with the explanation framework.

At this point, we would like to introduce two essential features that are critical to consider when examining your curriculum for existing tasks, or developing new ones, that are appropriate for scientific explanation: *data* and *scientific principles.* Keeping these features at the forefront of your planning will help you design tasks that involve students in constructing responses that align with the claim, evidence, reasoning framework.

Scientific Data

Whether students are discussing or writing scientific explanations, the learning task must include data and must require students to make sense of it. At its core, science is about using evidence to explain the world around us. Therefore, students must have access to data, either through firsthand data collection or some other means, to analyze and consider as evidence for their explanations in science. Returning to the kindergarten example from the beginning of the chapter, the lessons planned by Ms. Carpenter and Dr. Zeeland required students to answer the question, *What do seeds need to start growing?* In order to construct a scientific explanation to answer this question, students collected and recorded data (in the form of drawings and photographs of their observations) (see Figure 3.1) during an investigation in which they planted lima beans in dry and damp soil, as well as in plastic bags with a damp and a dry paper towel. In this example, students developed an explanation that responded to the question using data they had collected and analyzed themselves.

In some instances, especially in upper elementary grades, there may be science topics for which students cannot collect data, either because the topic does not lend

FIGURE 3.1

Recorded Observations for Kindergarten Seed Investigations

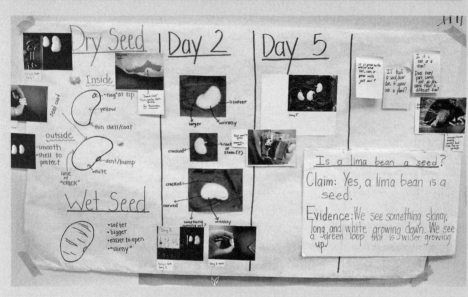

itself to an appropriate level of scientific investigation (e.g., solar system and space travel) or because of issues of scale. For example, topics such as dinosaur extinction do not allow for data collection because of the nature of the relevant evidence and time scale issues. Other topics, such as matter being composed of small particles called atoms, exist on a scale too small to examine directly in the classroom. These topics can still be appropriate for scientific explanation, but they require providing students with existing data sets to analyze or having them do research to determine what evidence scientists use to support their claims. Regardless of the case, if students are to be successful in constructing explanations in science, they need access to appropriate data.

Whenever possible, we recommend providing opportunities for students to collect data themselves as part of science instruction focused on explanation building. Having direct experience with the phenomena they are learning about and collecting data firsthand is both motivating and age appropriate for young learners. Furthermore, engaging students in firsthand experiences, coupled with the use of scientific language, can provide English language learners with an important foundation for learning both science and literacy. The real objects and experiences provide important concrete representations of the language for students (Olson et al., 2009). The interactions between students during investigations can also facilitate engaging all students in conversation, including those who struggle with literacy (Keenan, 2004). In addition, research suggests that for teachers who are learning to implement the explanation framework, taking on learning tasks that allow for data collection on the part of students is critical to successfully teaching science in this way (Barreto-Espino, 2009). Because engaging students in designing and conducting science investigations to collect the evidence necessary for explanation building is so fundamental to this approach to science teaching, we devote specific attention to it in Chapter 5.

Scientific Principles

The second feature of learning tasks to consider when planning for scientific explanation is *alignment with scientific principles.* As mentioned previously, science inquiry practices should be intertwined with science content (NRC, 2000). As described in the TIMSS Video Study (Roth et al., 2006), learning tasks should be content-rich, not content-free, and should require students to use science principles to answer questions and make sense of the physical world. Chapter 2 described the CER framework (claim, evidence, reasoning) within which the reasoning component involves using science principles to create a rationale for how or why the evidence supports the claim. Constructing explanations in science provides students with practice in applying principles they already know and helps them develop understanding of new principles. For instance, in the seed example, students applied their understanding of plants as living organisms and the requirements for living things to inform the investigation of water as a requirement for starting the growth of seeds. They used observation data and scientific principles to construct an explanation and to answer the guiding question. Moreover, their understanding was extended to include that water is a necessary condition for growth, but soil is not (at least not initially).

Previously we discussed that reasoning may not be an appropriate part of scientific explanations developed by young children. Even if you do not specify scientific principles that children will be required to apply as part of their explanations, identifying the science ideas associated with learning tasks will ensure that science content is a fundamental aspect of the learning tasks you use in your classroom. Recall that without being clear about the science concepts underlying your instruction, it is easy to fall into the trap of selecting fun activities that may not help develop important science ideas.

By keeping the two essential features—data and scientific principles—in mind when planning for science explanation, you will have a robust lens for evaluating existing learning tasks in your curriculum and/or designing new ones. For young learners, the preference is to create opportunities for them to grapple with data that they collect themselves. However, data can be provided in cases where opportunities for data collection are not available. You should keep the scientific principles that students will use or develop as they answer focus questions, at the forefront of your mind when planning.

In science instruction, we call learning goals that include the development of a scientific explanation *learning performances.* Learning performances address both the science content and the scientific inquiry practice, such as scientific explanations, to designate what students should be able to do (Krajcik, McNeill, & Reiser, 2008; McNeill & Krajcik, 2008b). Learning performances extend beyond stating a key science concept, such as the definition of a seed, to articulate how students should be able to apply that knowledge in context. Figure 3.2 provides an example of a learning performance for the content of seeds and the inquiry practice of explanation building for kindergarten.

The example in Figure 3.2 shows how the learning performance for students combines content with the CER framework in a way that specifies what the claim and evidence looks like for content associated with seeds. Other aspects of scientific inquiry, such as designing a fair test, can be used to develop learning performances. Learning performances will be addressed in more detail in Chapter 6 in which we discuss the development of assessment items for scientific explanation. Our main reason for raising the issue of learning performances here is that it explicitly allows for students to participate in constructing scientific explanations as part of instruction. When learning goals do not account for these kinds of performances, then it is easy for them to fall by the wayside in the hectic life of the classroom. Intentionally considering each lesson in terms of whether it is appropriate to combine content with inquiry ensures that students will have opportunities to engage in investigation and explanation.

In order to illustrate the importance of a coherent content storyline and planning for learning performances that connect science content and inquiry practices, we discuss a variety of focus questions and learning tasks that are appropriate for using the explanation framework with K–5 children. These examples are from different science

FIGURE 3.2 Structure of a Learning Performance

Content Standard	$\times$	Scientific Inquiry Standard	=	Learning Performance
A seed is the part of a plant that contains the baby plant (embryo) with its protective coat and stored food that can develop into a new plant under proper conditions. *National Life Science Standards for K–4, Life Cycles and Characteristics of Organisms* (NRC, 1996, p. 129)		*National Inquiry Standards for K–4, ...using data to construct a reasonable explanation* (NRC, 1996, p.122)		Students construct a scientific explanation that includes a claim about how water is a necessary factor for seeds to begin growing, and evidence in the form of observations that seeds grow in damp conditions (with or without soil).

disciplines and demonstrate that students can construct science explanations in biology, physical science, and earth and space science. Table 3.2 summarizes the examples by content and grade level, focus questions used to organize learning tasks and create a content storyline, and the learning performances that characterize the kinds of explanations that students are expected to develop. The kindergarten example is from Ms. Carpenter's class, which we have been discussing throughout the chapter. The other four examples are presented in the chart, and then elaborated on in the text that follows. Emphasis is placed on the kinds of evidence students need to support their claims.

The examples that follow illustrate the planning process underlying a variety of lessons of different content and grade levels. Because of the dynamic interplay between planning and teaching, some information about the implementation of the lesson is provided. The purpose of this approach is to illustrate how the content storyline and the CER framework provide ongoing guidance for instruction.

First- and Second-Grade: Sound[1]

The learning goal that Mrs. Kyle wanted the students in her first/second-grade split class to investigate was how sound is produced by vibrating objects. She worked on her content storyline by writing out the claim and evidence she wanted her students

TABLE 3.2 Examples of Focus Questions and Associated Learning Performances

Content Area and Grade Level	Focus Questions	Learning Performance
Kindergarten Biology: Seeds	What does a seed need to start growing?	Students construct a scientific explanation that includes a claim about how seeds need water to start sprouting and evidence in the form of observations of lima beans planted in wet/dry soil and in baggies with wet/dry paper towel.
1st and 2nd Grade Physics: Sound	What happens when an object makes a sound?	Students construct a scientific explanation that includes a claim about how vibrating objects can produce sound, and evidence in the form of observations of vibrations from a variety of sound-producing objects.
3rd and 4th Grade Earth Science: Water Cycle	What variables affect how quickly water evaporates on a chalkboard?	Students construct a scientific explanation that includes a claim comparing how temperature and wind increase the rate of evaporation and evidence from a data chart indicating the rate of evaporation under a variety of conditions.
5th Grade Earth Science: Day and Night Physics: Shadows	What direction do shadows move throughout the day? What direction does the earth rotate?	Students construct a scientific explanation that includes a claim about the direction that shadows rotate throughout the day and the direction of the earth's rotation, and evidence from recording their shadows in the morning, at midday, and afternoon and observing the same shadow rotation on a globe.

[1]Note that this is an extension of a basic lesson on sound from kindergarten (see video clip 5.5).

to develop from the investigations. Mrs. Kyle then developed the focus questions that would help her students construct that claim (Table 3.3), as well as a second claim that supported the first one, in addition she gave her students more evidence to connect sound and vibration.

By looking at her content storyline, Mrs. Kyle was able to set up the learning tasks to help her first- and second-graders construct scientific explanations about sound. She set up several stations using a variety of sound-producing objects so her students would have multiple representations of the concept she wanted them to understand. The stations included tuning forks, several different-sized drums with rice, a Tibetan singing bowl, and guitars (one commercially made and one homemade with a box and rubber bands). As the students rotated through the stations, Mrs. Kyle asked the students some questions: *What do you see happening when you are making sounds? What do you feel when you are holding the singing bowl? When does the sound stop?* A few students used the word *vibration* to explain what they were seeing and feeling, and Mrs. Kyle picked up on the term and began to use it in her small-group discussion with the class.

After the students had explored all of the sound-producing objects, Mrs. Kyle gathered the class together to talk about their observations. Many students shared that they felt and saw vibrations at the stations. Several students demonstrated how the objects made sound and the vibrations that were made when they struck or plucked the objects. Mrs. Kyle asked the question, *Can we make a claim about what happens when an object makes sound?* The students replied that sounds are made when objects vibrate. They provided evidence for the claim from the stations.

TABLE 3.3 Questions, Claims, and Evidence Chart for First- and Second-Grade Sound Lessons

Focus Question	Claim	Evidence
What happens when an object makes a sound?	The object vibrates when it make a sound.	We saw the tuning forks move back and forth (or vibrate) to make sounds. We put water in the sound bowl and it vibrated and made a sound when we hit the bowl. We saw the rice "jump" from the vibrations on the drums.
What happens to the sound when you stop the vibration?	When the vibration stops, the sound stops.	We touched the tuning fork to the table. It stopped vibrating and the sound stopped. We put our hands on the singing bowl to stop the vibrating and the sound stopped. When we stopped hitting the drum, the rice stopped jumping and the sound stopped.

Mrs. Kyle recorded the claim and supporting evidence on a class chart. Next, she asked the students if they noticed when the sound stopped. The students were not quite sure how to discuss this idea, so Mrs. Kyle decided that during the next lesson she would have the students intentionally stop the vibrations so they could make a clear claim about what happened when the sound stopped.

For the next lesson on sound, students were instructed to strike or pluck the sound-producing objects and then to touch the objects again to stop the vibrations, or, in the case of the drums, to hit them rapidly and then stop. Mrs. Kyle asked them to observe and listen carefully to what happened to the sound when they touched the vibrating object or stopped hitting the drums. After the students rotated through the stations again, they gathered to share their observations and make another scientific claim about sound. Following their explorations, the students were easily able to make the claim that the sound stops when the vibrations stop and they had multiple pieces of evidence to support their claim. The class went on to investigate pitch and volume.

Third- and Fourth-Grade: Water Cycle

Mrs. Gomez planned an earth science unit on the water cycle. Her main learning goal for the first lesson of the unit was for her students to know that part of the water cycle involves evaporation, which occurs when liquid water changes into its gas form as water vapor. Evaporation can be sped up through warm temperatures and wind. Mrs. Gomez's content storyline chart for the lesson included the claim and evidence shown in Table 3.4.

Mrs. Gomez set up a series of stations to help her students investigate the rate of evaporation and collect data to have numerical evidence to answer the focus question. The stations included small chalkboards, a fan, a heat lamp, a hair dryer, timers, bowls of water, and Q-tips®. The students rotated in groups through the

TABLE 3.4 Question, Claim, and Evidence Chart for Third- and Fourth-Grade Evaporation Lessons

Focus Question	Claim	Evidence
How can we speed up the rate of evaporation?	Using wind and heat caused evaporation to occur more rapidly.	When we timed how long it took a water line to evaporate from a chalkboard, we found that using a hairdryer (wind and heat) made the water evaporate in 5 seconds, whereas the heat alone took 8 seconds, and the fan (wind) alone took 10 seconds. The control (no wind, no heat) took 45 seconds to evaporate.

different stations so they could time the rate of evaporation at each station. At three of the stations, the students conducted multiple trials for the evaporation rate of the fan, heat lamp, and hair dryer. At the fourth station, the students timed the rate of evaporation without heat, wind, or the combination. The results of the test were compiled into a chart so the class could compare results and look for patterns in the data. Mrs. Gomez asked the students to discuss what happened to the water they put on the chalkboards. She wanted to make sure that students understood that the water did not just disappear, but rather it changed from a liquid to a gas called *water vapor.* She asked the students to help her write a definition of *evaporation* on their class chart under Scientific Principles. The class definition was "Evaporation happens when water changes from a liquid into a gas, becoming water vapor in the air." Mrs. Gomez asked her students to write a scientific explanation to answer their focus question and to use evidence and scientific reasoning to support their claim. Most of the students were able to write an explanation that looked similar to this:

> *Evaporation can be increased if you use heat and wind (CLAIM). When we used a hair dyer (heat and wind), the water on the chalkboard evaporated in 5 seconds. Heat by itself took 8 seconds, and wind (fan) took 10 seconds. The water took 45 seconds to evaporate by itself (EVIDENCE). The water on the chalkboard evaporated by changing from liquid water to water vapor in the air (REASONING).*

Fifth-Grade: Day/Night and Shadows

To help him plan a series of fifth-grade lessons on shadows that connected to unit concepts related to the earth's rotation, Mr. Rotz began by looking at the content storyline that he and his team of colleagues had developed. He saw that the learning goal for the students was to understand that shadows are made when an object blocks the path of light and that shadows change throughout the day because of the earth's rotation. Mr. Rotz wanted his students to investigate the focus questions: *How do shadows change throughout the day? What direction do shadows rotate throughout the day?* Next, he looked at the claims that he wanted his students to make about shadows and the earth's rotation, and he thought through the evidence he wanted his students to collect. Mr. Rotz planned to have his students go outside on a sunny day in the morning, at noon, and at the end of the school day to trace their shadows on the school playground or sidewalk with their partners. Students recorded how their shadow looked, measured and recorded the length, and noted the location of the sun for each shadow that was traced.

The following day, the class discussed the evidence they collected about their shadows. The students shared observations that shadows changed from longer, to smaller, and back to longer. The students looked at their recording sheets and noticed that the shadows rotated clockwise throughout the day. The class was able to make the claims shown in Table 3.5, based on evidence from their investigation.

TABLE 3.5 Claims and Evidence Chart for Fifth-Grade Lessons on Shadows (Part 1)

Claim	Evidence
Shadows change throughout the day by being long and thin in the morning, then shorter in the middle of the day, and longer again in the afternoon.	Most of our shadows were about 7 yards long in the morning, 3 yards long in the middle of the day, and 5 yards long at the end of the afternoon. (*Note:* The lengths will depend on the time of year and the latitude of the school.)
Our shadows rotated clockwise throughout the day.	When we looked at the direction the shadows moved, it was from left to right the same way that the clock moves.

Some students made observations about shadows and the sun. They noticed that the sun seemed to move through the sky and that the shadows appeared to be at an opposite angle from the sun. Mr. Rotz wrote the following questions on a class chart: *Does the sun really move through the sky during the day?* (Even though some students knew it did not, other students were not sure because the sun did appear to move during their shadow investigation.) *Are shadows formed in an opposite direction from the sun?* He told the class that they would investigate these questions over the next several days. As Mr. Rotz thought about his lesson for the next day, he decided to focus on the second question. He planned to have the students use pipe cleaner people and flashlights to try to simulate the way the shadows changed and moved outside.

Mr. Rotz realized that in order for the students to understand more about how shadows are made in relation to the location of the light source, the students needed to know the scientific principle that "light travels in a straight line." At the beginning of the lesson, he reminded the students of the red laser light traveling through a pan of red Jello™ they had observed in first grade. Mr. Rotz set up another representation of this principle by having a series of four index cards with a ¼-inch hole punched in the center. The cards were upheld up by modeling clay and placed 30 cm apart in a line on a table. Mr. Rotz turned off the lights and asked for volunteers to try to make the light from a flashlight travel through all the cards. He asked the students to notice what path the beam of light took. The students were able to observe that the light traveled in a straight line. "Light travels in a straight line" was added to the class chart under Scientific Principles.

Next, the students were instructed to take out their recording sheets from the previous day and they were asked to work in partners with a pipe cleaner person and their flashlights to try to match the shadows they recorded outside. The lights were turned off and the students placed their pipe cleaner person on the recording sheet and held the flashlight in various positions trying to match the shadows. As the students investigated, Mr. Rotz moved around, asking the students: *Where is the light when the shadow is slanted to the left? Where is the light when the shadow is slanted to the right? What do you notice about the position of the light and the*

Claim	Evidence
Shadows are formed on the other side of the person/object, opposite the light source.	When we held our flashlight on the right, the shadow was on the left. When we moved our flashlight to the left, the shadow was on the right.
Shadows are formed when an object blocks the light.	The pipe cleaner person blocked some of the light and we could see its shadow on our paper.

shadow? Can you make the shadow move by making one complete arc the way the sun appeared to move in the sky? The class gathered for a science talk about what they observed while trying to reproduce the shadows. Together the class decided they could add more claims with supporting evidence to the class chart (Table 3.6).

Mr. Rotz realized that with this lesson he could introduce the idea of scientific reasoning as a part of an explanation. He reviewed scientific explanations by asking students to name the parts of an explanation. The students responded, "Claim and evidence." Mr. Rotz asked the students to describe what a claim is and they answered, "The claim answers the question." Next, the students explained that evidence uses data or observations from the lesson to support the claim. Mr. Rotz told the class that he was going to add a third part to the explanation: scientific reasoning. He explained that reasoning helps to support the claim by including scientific principles or ideas that tell how or why the evidence supports the claim. He asked if there was a principle that they could use to help explain how shadows are formed. The students decided that "light travels in a straight line" could explain why shadows were formed opposite the light source. Together the class wrote a complete scientific explanation of their shadow investigation.

> *Shadows are formed when an object blocks the light (CLAIM). The shadow is formed behind the object opposite the light source because light travels in a straight line (REASONING). Our evidence for this claim is that when we held our flashlight on the right, the light traveled straight to the pipe cleaner person and was blocked, so a shadow formed on the left (EVIDENCE).*

When the class wrote their scientific explanation, they first provided a claim, then the reasoning that included the scientific principle, and finally the evidence from their investigation. Although we often refer to it as the CER framework, the components do not need to come in that order—claim, evidence, and reasoning. Rather, it is important that the components work together to form a coherent scientific explanation regardless of the order.

Taken together, these examples are intended to demonstrate how the CER framework can support planning as well as teaching. Having a clear sense of the learning goal for a lesson and unit allows you to shape a content storyline around questions and claims that are appropriate for your grade level. Activities and investigations that provide opportunities to collect the data necessary to construct those claims should be intentional. When possible, especially at upper grade levels, scientific principles that help further explain the connections between claim and evidence can be integrated, allowing for deeper scientific reasoning. Once you begin implementing your lessons, this planning approach provides a way to reflect on instruction in light of students' responses, questions, breakthroughs, and struggles. Being able to refer to your content storyline not only aids you in responding to ideas and issues that arise during instruction but it also serves as a constant reminder of next steps and potential connections among big ideas. Developing a coherent storyline that integrates scientific explanations can help all students develop a stronger understanding of the big ideas in science.

Complexity of the Learning Task

As students have more experiences with scientific explanations, they will become more proficient at coordinating claims, evidence, and reasoning. However, it is not reasonable to expect that you will be able to engage students in constructing explanations as part of every science lesson you teach. Learning tasks associated with these practices are best employed when students attempt to make sense of data/observations collected during the investigation of phenomena, which may occur only in an elementary classroom once a week or a couple of times each month. The trick is to identify places in your content storyline that lend themselves to scientific explanation, and then carefully design appropriate learning tasks for your students.

When designing learning tasks for scientific explanation, there are a number of modifications to the complexity or difficulty of the task that you can make to meet the needs of all the children in your class. Characteristics of the task that can affect its complexity for learners, such as openness of the question and type and amount of data, are shown in Table 3.7. The example draws on a learning task from Miss Carpenter's kindergarten class and their unit on seeds. Two variations on the task are provided that illustrate how characteristics of the task can be adjusted, making it more simple or complex.

Openness of the Question

Because engaging in scientific explanation requires crafting claims from evidence that answer a question about some phenomena, you may find phrasing the question to be a challenging activity. We certainly do! Our research also suggests that posing an appropriate question to frame investigation and explanation building is difficult for many practicing and preservice teachers (McNeill & Knight,

TABLE 3.7 Varying the Complexity of Characteristics of the Learning Task

Characteristic	Simple	Complex
Openness of question	Does water cause a seed to begin growing?	What does a seed need to begin growing?
Type of data	Observations of lima beans planted in soil plastic cups	Comparison of lima beans planted in soil and in baggies with a paper towel
Amount of data	9 lima beans in 2 conditions (6 cups total with 3 lima beans in each) Daily observations for 10 days	9 lima beans in 4 conditions (3 cups damp soil; 3 cups dry soil; 3 baggies with damp paper towel; 3 cups with dry paper towels)—each cup with 3 lima beans Daily observations for 20 days

in review; Zembal-Saul, 2010). By limiting the openness of the question, you can support younger students or those who are not experienced with scientific explanation. For example, posing a question that includes a potential claim can help students construct a claim that directly answers the question. For example, in Table 3.7, the simple version of the question is, *Does water cause a seed to begin growing?* The phrasing of the question limits the claim to two possibilities: Water causes a seed to start growing or water does not cause a seed to start growing.

After students have experienced constructing claims from evidence, a more complex question can be used. For example, in Table 3.7, the more complex question is, *What does a seed need to begin growing?* This question is more open in that students can now consider several factors related to initiating seed growth. It is a common idea among many young children that soil is necessary for a seed to start growing. In this case, Miss Carpenter created a situation in which students can notice a pattern with water (i.e., water is necessary for a seed to begin growing), but not for the material in which the seeds are placed (i.e., soil is not needed for seeds to begin growing). Students may also observe that too much water can cause seeds to rot. In other words, the openness of the question allows for students to construct more than one claim based on evidence from the investigation.

Characteristics of the Data

Another way to influence the complexity of the task is by making adjustments to the data that students collect and use to answer the question. When contemplating the large data set that students will generate during an investigation, it is important to consider the type and amount of data. Either or both features of the data set can be changed to vary complexity.

Type of Data. Students typically find it easier to deal with one type of data. In addition, quantitative data are more readily accepted as data than qualitative. Students may struggle to recognize qualitative data, such as observations, and fail to record it appropriately and notice patterns. In the example from Table 3.7, the type of data that students collect is qualitative, but can be altered to be more quantitative. For instance, in the simple variation, Miss Carpenter and her class decided that they would record data about the lima beans daily by marking a chart with an "✗" if there was no growth and a "✓" if there was. *Growth* was defined in advance as "something" emerging from the seed and poking up through the soil. In this way, a qualitative observation was recorded in a more concrete way, keeping the type of data simple and straightforward for young learners.

The more complex variation on data type for this investigation involves a comparison of lima beans planted in soil and those planted in plastic bags with a paper towel under wet and dry conditions. Because students were able to see the seeds in the bags, they were able to notice changes earlier than for those planted in the soil. They recorded changes in size, color, root development, and stem/ leaf development in their science notebooks. Miss Carpenter also documented the changes with photographs that they posted in the room and discussed. These data were more challenging to make sense of because they involved several different kinds of observations, none of which were straightforward to interpret. Nevertheless, guidance from the teacher allowed for productive sharing of observations and for using them to construct claims that answered the question.

Amount of Data. In addition to the *type* of data that students collect during an investigation, the *amount* of data can influence the complexity of the task. Even under the simple condition in this example, students collected a fair amount of data. Because Miss Carpenter wanted them to include "multiple trials" as a feature of their investigation, three lima beans were planted in each cup and three cups were planted for each condition (wet and dry). In other words, students were observing a total of six cups and eighteen lima beans and recording their observations across ten days. The more complex variation of the task significantly increases the amount of data by requiring four conditions (wet/soil, dry/soil, wet/ bag, dry/bag), each with three lima beans. Moreover, data are collected over a longer period of time so that students can begin to notice not just what a seed needs to start growing but how a seed grows into a plant, which is the next part of the investigation. Only one example is provided here, but the point is to recognize that the scientific explanation learning task can vary in complexity based on the data that are provided or the data that students collect.

Reasoning is not included as a separate component in Table 3.7 because it is dependent on the way the question is phrased and the data that students collect.

For example, reasoning about a simple task requires only a basic discussion: *Seeds need water to start growing. That is why the seeds in the damp soil had stems/leaves emerging after five days and nothing happened to the seeds in the dry soil even after ten days.* With the more complex task, students' reasoning includes scientific ideas related to the seed itself containing nutrients needed for plant growth: *Seeds need water to start growing, but they do not need soil. We noticed that the seeds in the cups with damp soil and the bags with damp paper towels had seeds that started to grow after a few days. The seeds in the dry soil and dry paper towels did not grow. The damp seeds grew without soil because the seed contained all of the nutrients necessary to get the baby plant off to a good start. Eventually, plants make their own food.* Varying the openness of the question and the complexity of the data determines the complexity of the reasoning.

Check Point

In this chapter, we focused on how to plan for instruction that incorporates scientific explanations to support all students in developing scientific literacy. A key aspect of that design includes developing a coherent science content storyline that focuses on the big picture, coherently sequences science ideas, and provides opportunities for explanation building. In order to identify opportunities in your curriculum where it makes sense to incorporate scientific explanations, you will want to consider two essential features: data and scientific principles. After identifying possible opportunities, you will then want to develop learning performances that explicitly combine the science content with the CER framework. This process will help you reflect on what it would look like for a student to construct a scientific explanation in either writing or talk.

Finally, you will want to consider the complexity of the learning task in terms of three characteristics: (1) openness of question, (2) type of data, and (3) amount of data. Varying these characteristics impacts the complexity of the scientific explanations that students construct. Working through this process and considering the different features and characteristics enables you to prepare science instruction that provides all students with opportunities to construct scientific explanations. In the next two chapters, we focus on other supports and instructional strategies that you can integrate into your lessons to help students in constructing scientific explanations. Then we shift our discussion to focus on assessment and how the CER framework can support the assessment of student learning in writing and talk.

Study Group Questions

1. Examine your existing science curriculum for opportunities for incorporating scientific explanations. Identify places that include the two essential features—data and scientific principles—that provide students with opportunities to justify claims with evidence and reasoning.

2. Design a learning task that considers the three characteristics that impact the complexity of the task (see Table 3.7): openness of question, type of data, and amount of data. For each of the characteristics did you design the task to be simple or more complex? Why did you make this decision?

3. Develop a coherent science content storyline for a science unit using a process similar to that used by Miss Carpenter and Dr. Zeeland. Create a planning matrix like Table 3.1 that highlights the questions, claims, evidence, and activities that you will include in your instruction.

Supporting Scientific Talk and Writing

Now that you have considered the key aspects of planning for scientific explanation in the classroom, what can you do to further support your students in talking and writing scientifically? In what ways does talk serve as a scaffold for younger children as they move toward writing explanations for science? How can you support students in constructing scientific explanations in talk in both whole-class and small-group discussions? How can you design writing scaffolds using the CER framework? In this vignette, fourth-grade teacher Mr. Park supports his students in successfully constructing a scientific explanation about air pressure by moving back and forth between investigation, small- and large-group discussion, and writing tasks. As you read, consider how each shift in activity contributes to the larger goal of explanation building.

As part of a unit on Air and Aviation in the beginning of the school year, Mr. Park wanted to introduce his fourth-grade students to the concept that air moving across a surface exerts less pressure than a static body of air. "When the children learn that concept," Mr. Park thought, "they could better understand part of the reason for lift on an airplane." The focus question for the investigation was: What happens when air moves across a surface? Mr. Park began by having his students go through a series of four investigations introducing Bernoulli's principle (an increase in the speed of moving air or flowing fluid is accompanied by a decrease in pressure). These tests included trying to blow a ping-pong ball out of a funnel, blowing across a strip of paper, blowing through a paper tent with a straw, and blowing between soda cans that were resting upright on a single layer of drinking straws. All the students believed they could blow the ball out of the funnel and were very surprised when it just spun around in the funnel cup. The results of the other tests were equally as counterintuitive, so Mr. Park had the students conduct the tests in a systematically structured investigation. In this way, they could predict and observe simultaneously and not give away the results. The students recorded their predictions, the procedures, and the results in their notebooks, as well as drew illustrations for each investigation. For each case, the students spent time talking about their predictions and then the results of what they observed.

After working through the four conditions, Mr. Park invited his students to meet as a group to discuss their ideas about what happens as air moves across a surface. The boys and girls reviewed each case and looked for patterns across the activities. Through guided discussion, the class came to the claim: Air moving over a surface is not as strong as still air or slower-moving air. *The students had multiple pieces of evidence to support the claim. For instance: "The cans moved toward each other when we blew air between them. The two sides of the paper tent moved together when we blew through it."*

Following the class discussion, the students returned to their notebooks and wrote explanations. Mr. Park provided writing scaffolds for each of the three components to remind the students what they needed to include in their scientific explanations. For example, the evidence scaffold stated: "Use data from each of the four investigations to support your claim about what happens when air moves across a surface." One student, Tannis, wrote: "Air moving across a surface is weaker than still air. My evidence for this is that we could not blow the ping-pong ball out of the funnel because the still air around it held the ball in the funnel."

As students finished their writing, Mr. Park invited them to share their explanations with the group and asked other students to provide feedback on the explanations. He asked the students, "Did you hear the claim and the evidence as you listened to the explanation? What feedback can you provide to help them improve their claim and evidence?" As students provided each other with feedback, he encouraged them to think about whether the claim explicitly answered the question and if the explanation included multiple pieces of evidence to support the claim. For example, when the class provided Tannis with feedback, the students thought she had written an excellent claim and included one very good piece of evidence, but she needed to include evidence from the other investigations as well.

Throughout this investigation, Mr. Park chose to structure a back-and-forth process of talking and writing. He knew that he would need to scaffold the lesson so that his students would have time to talk about what they were noticing and to record data and write explanations in their science notebooks. To help his students successfully navigate explanation building at this early point in the year, he guided them through the investigation step-by-step.

This vignette demonstrates the significance of thinking about talking and writing scientific explanations as intertwined. For younger learners, it is important to provide opportunities to talk about patterns of evidence and begin to shape explanations as a whole group before asking students to write a claim, evidence, and reasoning on their own. In this chapter, we elaborate on the interplay between talking and writing scientific explanations. In addition, we share approaches for facilitating whole-class discussions and small-group talk. Finally, we discuss scaffolds, visual representations, and other supports for helping all students construct written scientific explanations.

Interplay between Talking and Writing

The Common Core Standards for English Language Arts (Common Core State Standards Initiative, 2010) assert that students' writing should increase in sophistication from year to year in all aspects of language use, including the development and organization of ideas, as well as the ability to address demanding content. Engaging students in talking and writing scientific explanations is a complex practice that requires support as students learn how to participate in these practices. For young children who are new to writing explanations in science, whole-class discussion can serve as an important support. More specifically, we recommend that students come together as a whole group to discuss their predictions, share their data and examine them for patterns, and co-construct claims based on evidence *before* attempting to write about these things. After students are experienced with talking and writing explanations, the teacher can provide opportunities to engage students in writing independently or in small groups earlier in the process of explanation building.

Regardless of the sequence in which you choose to engage students in writing and talking about science ideas and experiences, the interaction between the two can be viewed as complementary and dynamic. The example we provide next is intended to highlight this dynamic interplay between talking and writing as it relates to constructing explanations from evidence. This science lesson occurs in a first-grade classroom at the end of the school year, and it is associated with the lesson on the factors affecting the period of a playground swing that will be described later in this chapter (video clip 4.3). It is important to note that the students have had a great deal of previous experience with data collection and constructing claims from evidence. In video clip 4.1, Mrs. Kur feels that by this time of the year her students are ready to work on writing scientific explanations on their own before coming together as a class to discuss the claims. The clip begins with her asking students to work in their small groups to write claims and evidence based on their data collection about swings. Mrs. Kur asks her students to clarify whether the short chain resulted in a shorter or longer swing time, then she encourages them to "get it down" on their papers.

After spending some time writing claims and evidence, the class gathers for a science talk about the explanations they wrote together in small groups. Mrs. Kur asks for a volunteer to share a claim that answers the question, *Does the length of the chain affect the time of swing?* One student contributes a claim that the teacher records, then she asks if other students would like to modify it or offer a claim that is phrased differently. Another student shares her claim that makes a statement about the swing times of both the long and short chains. Mrs. Kur requests that the students compare the two claims and several students share why they think that the second claim is "better." The first-graders engage in some debate about the claims. Their teacher helps them clarify that the second claim talks about both conditions rather than just one. At the end of the clip, Mrs. Kur asks her students to identify the evidence that they used to make their claim.

Although the video ends here, what follows is a summary of the rest of the lesson. The class goes on to discuss where they will find the evidence and then a student shares that the evidence is "right here on our papers." When Mrs. Kur asks the child to be more specific, she replies that it is in the data. Mrs. Kur asks students to look at their data sheets and decide whether it shows that the shorter chain corresponds to the shorter swing time. The students agree that the data support the same result even though each group has slightly different numbers. The class works together to write a statement with blanks that they can all complete using their own group's data. The statement looked like this: *The short chain took _____ seconds and the long chain took _____ seconds.* The students returned to their tables to work more on their individual written explanations.

Mrs. Kur clearly crafted this lesson to help her students make sense of their data

VIDEO 4.1

Writing Explanation

FIGURE 4.1

First-Grader's Written Explanation for Swing Time Investigation

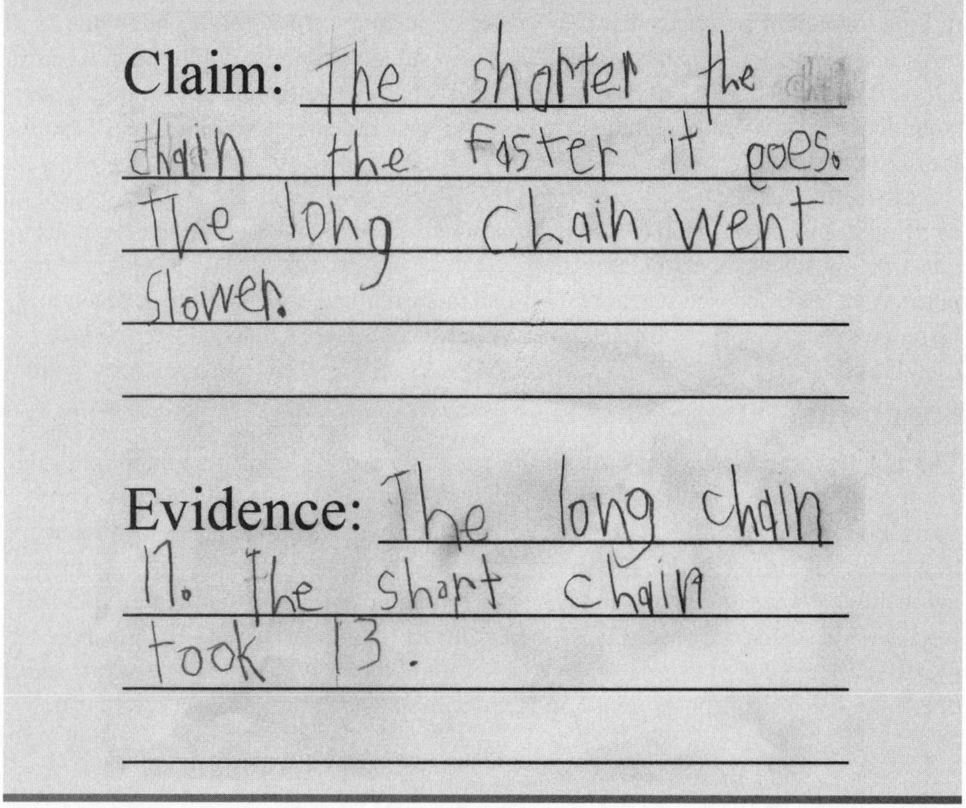

Claim: The shorter the
chain the faster it goes.
The long chain went
slower.

Evidence: The long chain
17. The short chain
took 13.

and construct evidence-based claims. Her progression from small-group writing to large-group discussion prepared her students to come to the class talk ready to share their data and ideas. More specifically, students moved through a sequence of small-group talk to small-group writing to large-group discussion, then back to individual writing. This investigation is an example of how talk and writing are intertwined in ways that assist students with building more robust explanations. The sample of one student's final written explanation (Figure 4.1) illustrates the power of this kind of process for young scientists.

In the sections that follow, we address ways in which the teacher can support students' scientific talk and writing. As you read about these approaches, we encourage you to keep in mind the complementary relationship between talking and writing, and to consider how you will use these ideas to support students' explanation building.

Scaffolding Scientific Talk

Scaffolds are supports that are intentionally designed to help learners engage in thinking and/or practices that they would be unable to successfully negotiate without assistance (Bransford et al., 2000). As students interact with scaffolds, they *learn* from them, becoming better able to engage in particular tasks. Eventually, as students are able to engage in tasks with less support, the teacher can remove the scaffolds. This is referred to as "fading."

Scaffolds can be supports provided by an individual, such as a teacher or peer, or by other resources, such as curriculum materials or technology. When it comes to constructing scientific explanations, there are several scaffolds that have been shown to improve students' and teachers' abilities to participate in this complex practice. Here we address supports for engaging in productive large- and small-group talk.

Supporting Whole-Class Discussion

The talk moves that a teacher uses during class discussion can play an important role in supporting the explanation building process. Here we address how teachers can use talk moves to scaffold students' communication of scientific ideas and evidence in ways that reflect scientific discourse. We also discuss how to make student thinking visible in order to identify and assess developments in understanding. In our work with teachers, we have found the talk moves outlined in *Ready, Set, Science!* (Michaels et al., 2008) to be a productive starting point for those who are new to class discussions that focus on evidence and explanation (see Table 4.1 for a summary).

TABLE 4.1 Talk Moves from *Ready, Set, Science!*

Talk Move	Question Example
Revoicing	So let me see if I've got your thinking right. You're saying _____?
Asking students to restate someone else's reasoning	Can you repeat what he just said in your own words?
Asking students to apply their own reasoning to someone else's reasoning	Do you agree or disagree and why?
Prompting students for further participation	Would someone like to add on?
Asking students to explicate their reasoning	Why do you think that? or What evidence helped you arrive at that answer? or Say more about that.
Using wait time	Take your time—we'll wait.

Source: Michaels et al., 2008, p. 91.

In the specific video clip we provide to illustrate talk moves (video clip 4.2), Ms. Hershberger gives a paper with six battery/bulb diagrams to her third- and fourth-grade students and asks them to predict whether the diagram will work to light the bulb. The students discuss their ideas during whole-class discussion. The teacher is surprised that a number of students are not sure about the diagram in which the wire is connected only to the bulb and not the bottom of the battery. All the students had worked in partners during the previous lesson where they were given a battery, bulb, and wire and found four ways to light the bulb. All four successful methods included both the positive and negative parts of the battery, and the students had sketched them in their science notebooks. Therefore, when some students started to say that the bulb might light without being connected to both the negative and positive ends of the battery, Ms. Hershberger decided it was important to hear more about their thinking. She used a series of talk moves to address multiple students and elicit their thinking.

VIDEO 4.2

Talk Moves

The clip begins with students discussing a diagram that they all agreed will not work, and one student explains his reasoning for why the bulb will not light. Ms. Hershberger moves to another diagram and the first student to respond thinks that it will work. He explains that as long as it is connected to the battery in some way, he thinks the bulb will light. The teacher asks if anyone agrees or disagrees with his ideas and one student quickly raises her hand to share her thinking about why she disagrees. The clip continues with Ms. Hershberger asking many students, "What do you think?" The students explain whether they think the configuration in the diagram will work and they share the reasons for their thinking. Four or five students think the bulb will light and a number of other students disagree with that prediction. The teacher asks, "How do you know that? Do you have any evidence to support that?" One student does not give a complete reason and is asked why several times. The reasoning that he eventually shares is: "I think it will work because it was like what we tested last time, it's just littler." [Meaning the diagram still has a circuit connecting the bulb and battery, it is just a smaller loop.] The prediction talk ends with a student suggesting that they test it, and Ms. Hershberger replies that they will test the configurations in the diagrams.

Ms. Hershberger found students' responses surprising because it seemed as though they should have known from the earlier lesson that both ends of the battery need to be connected for the electrical current to flow. However, as soon as she noticed that some students were not certain, she realized that it was important to take time to talk through their predictions and the reasons for their thinking.

By listening to their thinking, the teacher was reminded that students often need multiple opportunities to explore the phenomenon before their understanding of the concept is solidified. In addition, as she listened to the students explain their thinking she heard some misconceptions about energy and electrical current. She recognized that in future lessons, she would need to plan ways for the students to gain more scientific background and information to understand the concept of complete circuits, electrical current, and energy transformations.

We consider talk moves to be scaffolds because as learners become accustomed to being asked, *What's your evidence?,* they automatically begin to include evidence as part of their contribution to discussions. Over time, the teacher needs to ask the question less frequently and the scaffold fades over time. Similar observations have been made of students' use of agree/disagree language and their ability to weigh their reasoning against that of their peers. Most of the video clips that accompany Chapter 5 include attention to the talk moves described here. It may be a useful exercise to view some of these clips with particular attention to teacher questions and note the variety of ways in which the construction of scientific explanations is scaffolded.

Attending to Small-Group Talk

Talk moves are powerful scaffolds for making thinking visible and negotiating meaning in the context of whole-class discussion, and they can be modified when working with small groups of students. In addition to talk moves, there are a number of other supports to consider when working with small groups. In our work with teachers, we are frequently asked what small-group talk sounds like and how the teacher can help assist students' explanation construction during small-group work. Our experiences with elementary teachers have revealed that there is a tendency to focus on surface-level aspects of small-group interactions when teaching science (Zembal-Saul, 2009), especially during investigations. For example, we often see novice teachers moving from group to group, asking questions, such as *What are you doing? How is it going? Have you recorded your data/observations?* An emphasis on making procedural adjustments also is common—for example, helping students get materials or set up their equipment. In contrast, we challenge teachers to use the CER framework to inform the kinds of questions they ask as they visit small groups. The aim is to monitor and assess student thinking in order to support their sense making and explanation construction.

The CER framework can be used to guide teacher questions and supports in a number of ways (Table 4.2). Consider the importance of the questions around which explanation building is framed. When a small-group investigation is moving in an unanticipated direction that could result in a departure from the learning outcome of the lesson, drawing students' attention back to the guiding question can be an effective approach. Merely asking, *How does this help us*

TABLE 4.2 Using the CER Framework to Support Small Group Talk

CER-Informed Approach	Question Example
Refocus on the guiding question	How does that help us answer our question, _____?
Look for patterns in the data	What patterns are you beginning to notice in your data?
Make a draft claim	What claim can you make based on the data you have so far?
Consider alternatives	Is there a different claim that explains the data better?
Make new predictions	Given your results so far, what do you predict will happen next?

answer our question? can redirect students to the purpose of the investigation and data collection. A different approach to using the CER framework during small-group work is to encourage students to begin examining their data for patterns. Patterns in data often serve as a mechanism for making an informed prediction about what might happen next or as precursors to the development of evidence-based claims. Consider, for instance, Ms. Hershberger's battery and bulb lesson. Prior to the whole-class discussion about circuit diagrams, students investigated a variety of configurations of the battery, bulb, and wire. As students worked in teams, Ms. Hershberger went from group to group, asking them to identify patterns across the configurations in which the bulb did and did not light. Some students noticed that two parts of the base of the bulb and both positive and negative ends of the battery needed to be attached in order for the bulb to light. This became the basis of a claim about complete circuits.

Another important reason to focus on monitoring and assessing student thinking during small-group work is to gain insight into where students are struggling in ways that might negatively impact the development of the scientific explanation and to consider how you might help. In video clip 4.3, Mrs. Kur has divided her first-graders into small groups to collect data around the question, *What things will affect how long or short the swing ride will be?* The students are testing the length

VIDEO 4.3
Student Thinking

of the chain, a large angle of release versus a much smaller angle, and the weight of the washers on the chain. The three students in each group all have roles: timer, counter, and recorder. Mrs. Kur has asked her students to do three trials so that they will have more accurate data. As the students are working in their groups, Mrs. Kur is circulating around the class and checking to see how the students are making sense of the data they are collecting.

In the video, students are counting the number of swings and then recording on their data charts the amount of time it takes. In one of the small groups, Mrs. Kur notices that students do not really understand that a greater number of seconds equates to a slower "time" or speed. More specifically, when she questions the group about what their data mean, the students say that the longer time means the swing ride is faster. Mrs. Kur realizes that it is important to address this issue in order for students to eventually be able to make accurate claims. She asks them to think about running and provides a scenario in which she runs down the hall in 15 seconds and a student runs down the hall in 20 seconds. Mrs. Kur asks the students who would have the faster time. "You would!" the students answer simultaneously. Mrs. Kur then reminds her students that the bigger the number, the slower the speed, and then she revisits the chain with the large angle of release (long pull back) and asks if this pull makes the swing go faster or slower. The students modify their response appropriately in light of the example. Mrs. Kur asks them to conduct two more trials so they will have more data. Following additional data collection, the teacher returns to the small group to ask students an informal assessment question. She challenges them to determine what the angle of release should be (long pull back or a short pull back) if they intend to produce a long ride on the swing. The students use data from their investigation to answer that a long pull would give a nice long ride.

This video clip illustrates the importance of teachers listening to students as they engage in small-group investigations. As a teacher circulates from group to group during investigations, it is important to ask various types of questions to help understand students' thinking—and in particular to identify struggles that have the potential to interfere with meaning making and explanation building. Assessing and monitoring student thinking by asking questions based on the CER framework, such as *What do your data mean? How do these data answer our question? What are you finding?* provide opportunities for teachers to reveal what their students are thinking and to consider ways to support them. Especially at lower elementary grades, students are often confused about what the numerical data they gather actually mean. Frequently, younger students think that larger numbers are "better," as we saw in the video. Teachers need to be diligent listeners as they support their students to make sense of the data that will be used to make claims. It may be tempting to try to explain what the numbers mean before students have undertaken the investigation; however, our experience suggests that this has little meaning to students. We have found that addressing the meaning of numerical data in the context of the investigation provides purpose for understanding the data as evidence.

By visiting small groups with the goal of assessing and monitoring their thinking, the teacher can use what she or he learns to foster improved participation in whole-group discussion. Small-group interactions create a vehicle for attending to an individual student's ideas in ways that are challenging to ascertain during whole-class discussion. In our work in classrooms we often see some children who are reluctant to participate in large-group discussion; however, they are actively engaged in sharing their ideas during small-group work. We encourage teachers to listen carefully to the contributions of these children and to approach them about sharing specific ideas with their classmates during discussion. For example, in Miss Carpenter's kindergarten class (see Chapter 3) there was a little girl, Amy, who rarely talked in whole-class settings. During one of the seed lessons, she noticed that the leaves appeared to emerge from the lima bean seed (cotyledon) that was still attached to the developing plant. She was able to make connections back to early observations of the inside of the seed to a structure the class had referred to as a "flag" (first leaves). Miss Carpenter heard her talk about this in the small group and asked her to share her observation with the whole class during the discussion. In this way, Amy's idea was validated and she was prepared and confident when it came time to communicate her thinking with the class. Her evidence was an important part of developing a claim about how seeds grow into plants.

Small-group discussion can be an effective tool for supporting all students in scientific explanations. Previous research suggests that group interaction is a key component of effective instruction for English language learners (Pray & Monhardt, 2009). Working in groups allows students to practice using science language with their peers and to observe their peers using science language, which provides another model of language use in addition to their teacher. Collaborative group work supports both science learning and language learning (Keenan, 2004). Small-group interactions can be an effective tool for teachers to monitor and assess their students' learning and for students to provide each other with valuable support.

Supports for Scientific Writing

Scientific talk is an important tool to support students in writing explanations because it provides students with an opportunity to engage in scientific discourse, as well as receive oral support from their teacher and classmates. In addition, different written scaffolds and visual representations can provide support to help students appropriately justify their claims in writing. These supports can be provided to all students to help them in this complex practice or they can be individualized in order to address the needs of specific students in your classroom. Using visual supports can help all students, including individuals with linguistically diverse backgrounds or special needs, succeed in this complex practice of constructing scientific explanations. For example, the SIOP (sheltered instruction observation protocol) model recommends using visual aides, graphic organizers, and other types of representations to support English language learners across the content areas (Echevarria, Vogt, & Short, 2008). Visual representations are also an important strategy for supporting students with special needs, particularly for students with difficulty in processing and reading comprehension (Steele, 2007). Providing multiple types of support in your classroom offers students different opportunities to receive the help they need to engage in scientific explanations. In the next section, we describe how to design writing scaffolds, visual representations, and other supports that utilize the claim, evidence, and reasoning framework.

Writing Scaffolds

As we mentioned previously, a *scaffold* is a temporary support provided by a teacher, curriculum, or other tool that allows a student to accomplish a practice that he or she could not do independently (Bransford et al., 2000). Writing scaffolds for scientific explanations are sentence starters, questions, or other prompts that provide students with hints about what to include in their scientific explanations. *Sentence starters,* or sentence frames, can be an effective strategy for supporting English language learners, because the students do not have to focus on how to formulate the beginning of the sentence (Nelson, 2010). Instead, they can focus on the key science ideas they want to include in their writing. Writing scaffolds can be directly typed on students' data recording sheets or they can be displayed on a board or with a projector for students to use as they are writing in their science journals. When we design writing scaffolds, there are four characteristics that we consider: (1) general and content support, (2) detail and length, (3) fading, and (4) structure (see Table 4.3).

General and Content Support. When designing writing scaffolds, we typically consider whether to include general and content specific support for each of the components. General support provides hints about the framework that could be used in any content area. Content-specific support provides hints about the specific content or task that the students are trying to answer. In order to illustrate the difference, we will use an example that we designed for a fifth-grade unit focused on adaptations. Figure 4.2 shows the results and conclusion section of a student sheet we designed for an investigation addressing the following question, *Which "bird beak" is the best adaptation for each specific food?* In this investigation, students worked in groups of four with each student responsible for one of four simulated bird beaks—chopsticks, spoon, tweezers, and straw. The fifth-graders held a competition to discover which bird beak could best "eat" each of four "food" sources (marbles, pennies, popsicle sticks, and red water). The students had one minute to move as much so-called food as they could from the original source to their "stomachs," which were clear plastic cups. After competing

TABLE 4.3 Characteristics of Writing Scaffolds

Characteristics	Description
General and Content Support	• General support provides hints about the scientific explanation framework that could be used in any content area (e.g., Evidence is scientific data). • Content support provides hint about the specific content or task the students are trying to answer (e.g., Evidence should include the amount of food that the beaks ate).
Detail and Length	• Students with less experience with the framework may benefit from longer scaffolds with more detail. • Students with lower English language proficiency (e.g., younger students or ELLs) may need shorter scaffolds in order to minimize the reading demands.
Fading	• As students gain more experience with the framework, the level of detail should decrease.
Structure (explanation, sentence starter, or question)	• Different structures may work better depending on the experiences of your students. An explanation is a description of the component. A sentence starter provides students with part of a sentence. A question provides a hint to consider for the specific component.

for each food source, the students filled in the corresponding column in the data table. When they finished collecting data, the students wrote a scientific argument addressing the overarching question of which beak is the best adaptation for each specific food.

The scaffold for evidence in Figure 4.2 includes both general and content-specific support. The first sentence, which states, "Provide scientific data to support your claim," includes general support for evidence that could be used in any content area. The second sentence in the scaffold, which states, "The evidence should include the amount of food (marbles, pennies, popsicle sticks, and red water) that the birds with the adapted beaks ate," provides content-specific support for the particular investigation that the students completed. In our previous research (McNeill & Krajcik, 2009), we found that students' written scientific explanations showed the greatest gains when they received both general support for the framework and content-specific support that explained how to use the framework in a particular context. Students need to develop a general understanding of the framework, but they must also know how to apply the framework to the different data they analyze. For example, they need to understand what counts as evidence when they are explaining adaptations versus erosion versus phase changes. Consequently, when we designed the writing scaffold for the adaptation investigation, we included both general and content-specific support.

FIGURE 4.2

Writing Scaffold for Adaptation Investigation

Results

Beak	Marbles	Pennies	Popsicle Sticks	Red Water
Chopsticks				
Spoon				
Tweezers				
Straw				

Conclusion:
[Write an argument that answers the question: Which bird beak is the best adaptation for this environment?]

Claim
[Write a sentence stating which bird's beak is the best adaptation for this environment.]

Evidence
[Provide scientific data to support your claim. The evidence should include the amount of food (marbles, pennies, popsicle sticks, and red water) that the bird with the adapted beak ate.]

Reasoning
[Explain why your evidence supports your claim. Describe what an adaptation is and why your evidence allowed you to determine which bird beak was the best adaptation.]

Detail and Length. Another characteristic that we consider when designing writing scaffolds is the level of detail and the length of the scaffold. In deciding on the level of detail and length, we take into consideration the background of the students. First of all, if students have less experience with the framework, they can benefit from longer scaffolds, which include more detail. For example, we designed the writing scaffolds in Figure 4.2 for fifth-graders who had been introduced to the framework before, but were still relatively new at writing scientific explanations. Consequently, we felt it was important to remind them of the general definitions of the components—such as reasoning explains why your evidence supports your claim.

Another background characteristic of students to consider in designing writing scaffolds is the students' level of English language proficiency. Students with less English language proficiency, such as younger students or English language learners, may need shorter written scaffolds in order to minimize the reading demands. Including a lot of written detail in the scaffolds may actually overwhelm the students instead of providing clarification for the particular component. For example, one of the second-grade teachers that we worked with included only the words *claim* and *evidence* after the question in order to remind his students to include these two components. He believed that including additional text would have been too much for his students. Instead, he created icons to go along with *claim* and *evidence,* which he included on the student sheet. Next to *claim,* he included a question mark to remind students to answer the original question. Next to *evidence,* he included an image of a student looking through a magnifying glass to remind students to use their observations and measurements as evidence. In this case, instead of using detailed text defining the components, he used images as visual reminders of the definitions they had created as a class.

Fading. Scaffolds are defined as "temporary" supports with the idea that students should eventually be able to complete the task without the additional support. Initially receiving detailed support can help students develop a stronger understanding of the framework. However, if the detail continues indefinitely, students might not learn the appropriate way to justify their claims in writing on their own. We conducted research comparing two groups of middle school students during a chemistry unit (McNeill et al., 2006). One group of students received detailed support for every investigation; the other group received support that was less detailed, or faded, over time. We found that students who received the faded written scaffolds were able to write stronger scientific explanations in which they appropriately justified their claims.

The results from this study suggest that it can be important to fade the support you provide students over time to help them internalize the framework and be able to apply it to new situations. For example, if the scaffolds in Figure 4.2 were designed for students with more experience in writing scientific explanations, we would have included less detail. In the evidence scaffold, instead of having two separate sentences for the general and content-specific support, these could have been combined

TABLE 4.4 Three Structures for Writing Scaffolds

	Explanation	Sentence Starter	Question
Claim	Write a sentence stating which beak is the best adaptation for this environment.	The _____ beak is the best adaptation for this environment.	What beak is the best adaptation for this environment?
Evidence	Provide scientific data to support your claim. The evidence should include the amount of food (marbles, pennies, popsicle sticks, and red water) that the birds ate.	My evidence to support my claim is that the bird with the _____ beak ate _____ marbles, _____ pennies, _____ popsicle sticks, and _____ red water. This is better compared to the other birds that ate _____.	What scientific data do you have to support your claim? How much food (marbles, pennies, popsicle sticks, and red water) did the birds with different beaks eat?
Reasoning	Explain why your evidence supports your claim. Describe what an adaptation is and why your evidence allowed you to determine which bird beak was the best adaptation.	An adaptation is _____. My evidence supports my claim that the _____ beak is the best adaptation because _____ _____.	Why does your evidence support your claim? What is an adaptation and how do you know which beak is the best adaptation?

into one shorter sentence, such as "Provide scientific data that include the amount of food the birds with adapted beaks ate." Or if the students had a lot of experience, the scaffold could just state "Evidence—consider the amount of food" to provide a general reminder to include evidence and a specific prompt about what counts as evidence. As students develop a more in-depth understanding of how to justify their claims in science, they need less detailed scaffolds to support them in their writing.

Structure. The last characteristic we consider of the writing scaffolds is their structure in terms of whether we design them as an explanation, sentence starter, or question. An *explanation* provides a description of the component. A *sentence starter* provides students with a template to complete in their writing. Finally, a *question* provides a hint to consider for the specific component. The decision between the three different styles depends on the experiences of the teacher and the students. All three structures can convey similar information, just in a different format. The scaffolds included in Figure 4.2 provided an explanation for each of the components. In Table 4.4, we illustrate how these scaffolds could be modified to include the structure of a sentence starter or a question. Similar to what we described before, the level of detail in the three structures can be modified to include

FIGURE 4.3

Classroom Poster of Scientific Explanation

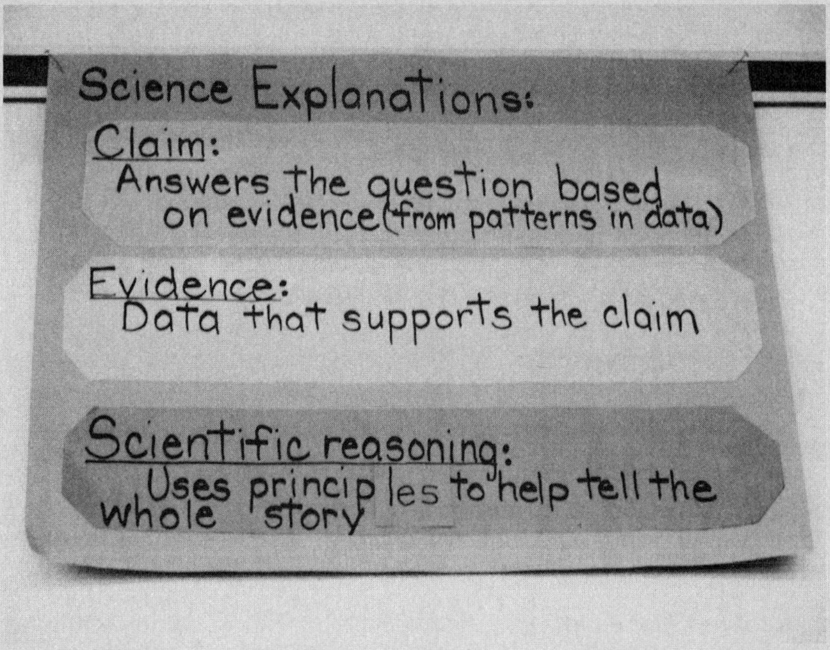

more or less detail depending on the backgrounds of the students in terms of both their experience with the framework and their level of English language proficiency.

Scaffolds can provide a visual support to help students appropriately justify their claims in writing. In designing the scaffolds, you may wish to take into consideration, including general and content support, the level of detail and length, fading the support over time, and what structure would be most effective in your classroom. Also, you might use the same writing scaffolds for all your students or you might want to individualize them to meet the needs of specific students.

Visual Representations

Creating a classroom poster or other visual representation to post on the classroom wall can serve as a visual reminder to students of how to construct a scientific explanation. The poster can be as simple as listing the different components or providing definitions for each of the components. For example, Figure 4.3 illustrates one example in which claim, evidence, and reasoning are each defined. Posters such as this one can be created as part of an initial lesson introducing the framework or added later on as a reminder of what the class has already discussed.

In addition, the poster can include visuals, such as the icons we mentioned before developed by a second-grade teacher (claim—a question mark; evidence—a student looking through a magnifying glass). Posters can also be added to or revised over the course of the school year. For example, if you initially introduce only claim and evidence, you could start with those two components and then add reasoning later on in the school year. Another possibility would be to add specific examples to the poster as you address different science topics during the school year. For instance, if you introduced the framework during a unit on simple machines, you might include examples of evidence such as distances and forces. Then if your next unit focused on biodiversity, you could add other examples of evidence such as numbers of species and descriptions of adaptations (such as color). The visual should serve as a resource for students to help them understand how to justify their claims in science writing.

Other Writing Supports

In addition to writing scaffolds and posters, the teachers we work with have designed a number of other creative strategies to help their students write stronger scientific explanations. Specifically, we describe two examples that have worked well to support students who were struggling with different aspects of the scientific explanation framework.

Debating Multiple-Choice Options. As students gain experience in writing scientific explanations, they can develop an understanding that they need to justify their claims with evidence and reasoning. However, they can still struggle with what counts as strong evidence and strong reasoning. In order to help students evaluate the quality of different pieces of evidence and reasoning, we developed a strategy with one elementary teacher, Mr. Martin, in which students have to select and debate what counts as the strongest claim, evidence, and reasoning (McNeill & Martin, 2011). Figure 4.4 includes an example of this multiple-choice strategy. This example would be used after fourth-grade students conducted a number of experiments in which they tested how different variables impacted the speed of a parachute. The students would work in groups to select what they felt was the strongest claim, two pieces of evidence, and reasoning. The specific choices were designed to target common student difficulties with each of the components.

For the claim, Choice C is the appropriate choice, because it includes the specific size ($2,500 \text{ cm}^2$) and material (plastic bag) that the parachute would need to be built from in order to fall the slowest. Choice A was designed to include vague language, "the best materials," to illustrate the importance of including specific details in the claim. Choice B specifies that size and material are important, but it does not explicitly answer the question of how to make the parachute go the slowest. Debating and discussing these choices could help students understand the importance of including specific details and answering the question in the claim.

FIGURE 4.4

Multiple-Choice Student Sheet

Directions

You have just finished testing how different variables (size and material) affect the speed of a parachute. With your group, you need to create an argument that answers the following question: What design of a parachute will go the slowest? Circle the choices below that you think would create the strongest argument.

CLAIM

Circle ONE of the following.

    A. Our parachute will go the slowest because we will use the best materials.

    B. The size and the material cause a parachute to go slow or fast.

    C. A parachute that is 2,500 cm^2 and made out of a plastic bag will go the slowest.

EVIDENCE

Circle TWO of the following.

    A. We built many different parachutes and we tested them by timing how long it took for them to reach the ground.

    B. The parachute that was 2,500 cm^2 took 5.2 seconds to hit the ground, whereas 1,600 cm^2 took 4.1 seconds, 900 cm^2 took 3.6 seconds, and 400 cm^2 took 2.1 seconds.

    C. Real parachutes are made out of strong materials, like nylon, because they do not let any air go through the parachute, which makes them go slower.

    D. The parachute that was made out of the plastic bag took 4.3 seconds, whereas the construction paper took 3.5 seconds and the cotton took 2.7 seconds.

    E. Our experiments showed that the parachute that was the largest and the one made out of the plastic bag fell the slowest.

    F. We had a lot of fun building and testing the different parachutes because we got to try out many different ideas.

REASONING

Circle ONE of the following.

    A. Our data table shows how to build the slowest parachute. We found that the largest parachute fell slower compared to the other three parachutes. We also found that the parachute made out of a plastic bag fell slower compared to the parachutes made of construction paper and cotton.

    B. The parachute should be 2,500 cm^2 and made out of a plastic bag because those had the greatest air resistance. The largest parachute hit more air as it fell, so it went slower. The plastic bag did not let much air go through the materials, so it went slower. The more air resistance, the slower the parachute falls.

    C. Skydivers need to use parachutes so they can land on the ground safely. Gravity pulls them toward the earth and causes them to fall. We did experiments to find out what parachute would work best to keep a skydiver safe. We found that having a large parachute made out of plastic fell the slowest.

Evidence Choice B and Choice D provide the most appropriate evidence for the claim because they include specific data (i.e., time) for the different investigations that the students conducted. Choice A and Choice D were included to represent evidence that provides a general description of the experiment or results, but they do not include specific data. Choice C includes a real-life example that is relevant, but again it does not include specific data either from the investigation the students conducted or investigations someone else has conducted using nylon. Choice F illustrates text that focuses more on a personal narrative or story about why the students had "fun" conducting the investigation. Certainly, it is important for students to enjoy their science experiences, but this emotion does not help justify what design of a parachute will result in it traveling the slowest. Debating these different choices will help students understand the importance of including specific data in their evidence.

Finally, for reasoning, Choice B is the strongest because it explains why the evidence supports the claim using the "big idea" of air resistance. Choice A was included because it summarizes the evidence, but it does not include the big science idea. Choice C was included because it includes the science concept of gravity, but it does not explain why the evidence supports the claim. Debating these choices can help students understand these two different characteristics of strong reasoning—it explains why the evidence supports the claim and uses relevant science ideas to make that justification.

Ultimately, our goal is for students to be able to write their own scientific arguments in which they justify their claims with appropriate evidence and reasoning. Consequently, we do not recommend using only multiple-choice format. However, we have found that this format can support a productive discussion in which students debate the quality of the different choices for claim, evidence, and reasoning. (See video clip 4.11 in McNeill & Krajcik, 2012, for a different example and classroom discussion.) This strategy is another tool to support students in writing stronger scientific explanations.

Checking and Justifying Evidence. As we mentioned previously, students can struggle to understand what counts as strong evidence and reasoning in their scientific explanations. One of our teacher colleagues, Mr. Roberts, designed the student sheet in Figure 4.5 to help his second-graders think about appropriate evidence and reasoning. The students had been learning about insects in class and had developed a list of characteristics of insects, including: All insects have six legs, insects have exoskeletons, most adult insects have antennae, all insects have a life cycle with four stages, and most insects have wings. Mr. Roberts wanted the second-graders to use what they had learned about insects to determine what pieces of evidence could support the claim, "Yes, butterflies are insects." He purposefully included some choices that would require the students to think really hard about whether the evidence supported their claim. For example, "Butterflies have legs" is *not* evidence that a butterfly is an insect, but "Butterflies have six legs" is

FIGURE 4.5

Checking and Justifying the Evidence Student Sheet

Focus on Evidence and Reasoning

Question: Are butterflies insects?

Claim: Yes, butterflies are insects.

First, <u>check the boxes of all evidence</u> listed below that help support the claim.
Then, <u>write the reason</u> why that evidence helps support the claim.
If the evidence does not help support the claim, write "<u>not important evidence</u>."

Evidence: ☐ Adult butterflies have wings.

Reason: _____

Evidence: ☐ Adult butterflies have antennae.

Reason: _____

Evidence: ☐ Butterflies have many different colors on their wings.

Reason: _____

Evidence: ☐ Butterflies have legs.

Reason: _____

Evidence: ☐ Butterflies drink from flowers.

Reason: _____

Evidence: ☐ Butterflies have six legs.

Reason: _____

Evidence: ☐ A butterfly develops from an egg, caterpillar, and chrysalis.

Reason: _____

appropriate evidence for the claim. Making these choices encouraged the students to think about their reasons for why the evidence helps support the claim.

Writing scientific explanations can be challenging for students. In order to support students in this complex practice, there are a variety of different supports that can be designed to support all students. Providing students with multiple opportunities and multiple supports will enable them to construct stronger scientific explanations over time.

Supporting All Learners in Scientific Explanation

Throughout this chapter, we have discussed a variety of strategies to support all learners, including English language learners and students with special needs, in successfully engaging in scientific explanations. These strategies align with the recommendations from the Universal Design for Learning (UDL) framework (Rose & Meyer, 2002). The UDL stresses the importance of integrating the following into instruction in order to better support the needs of all learners: (1) multiple modes of engagement, (2) multiple modes of representation, and (3) multiple modes of expression. Designing science lessons using these three recommendations can make learning accessible for all students, including those with linguistically or culturally diverse backgrounds, sensory disabilities, or learning disabilities.

Multiple modes of engagement stress using a variety of strategies to motivate or interest students in learning a topic. For example, the vignette at the beginning of the chapter from Mr. Park's classroom included a focus question *(What happens when air moves across a surface?)* to introduce the topic, an investigation in which students conducted four tests, and both small-group and large-class discussions. Some of his fourth-graders may have been engaged by the initial focus question simply because they were interested in science or did not know the answer to the question. Other students may have been motivated by the experience of physically manipulating the materials during the science investigations or because the results of the investigations were counterintuitive. Finally, other students may have been motivated by working with their peers. Students become engaged in science for different reasons. Incorporating a variety of different engagement strategies into a lesson increases the chances that all students will be interested.

In order to help students develop a stronger understanding of scientific explanations, you need to represent the framework in many ways. Specifically, we have discussed different ways to orally and visually represent the framework to students. In terms of an oral description of the framework, this can come from the teacher, but it can also come from the students either in full-class discussions or in small-group discussions. For example, the language a teacher uses to explain what counts as evidence may be different for various students in the classroom. By hearing the components described in different ways, this may help students develop a more robust understanding of the framework. Furthermore, we discussed creating writing scaffolds to include on investigation sheets, posters, or representations to place on the classroom wall, and other supports (e.g., the multiple-choice selection of claim, evidence, and reasoning), all of which provide other visual representations of the framework. Utilizing these different representations provides a variety of access points for students if they did not understand the initial introduction of the framework.

Incorporating multiple modes of expression, such as talking, writing, and investigating, in science lessons provides students with a variety of ways to demonstrate their understanding, which allows all students, including those with special needs, to successfully participate in the science lesson (Britsch & Heise, 2006). Throughout the chapter, we discussed the important interplay between talking and writing. Using both modes of expression allows students different ways to express their understanding and provides you with more in-depth knowledge of the students' level of achievement. For example, if a student does not include evidence to support her claim in writing, yet she offered important evidence as part of the class discussion, this suggests that she understands the idea of evidence, but is having difficulty translating that understanding in her writing. Regarding writing, we specifically suggest some scaffolded strategies to aid students as they move toward greater independence. For instance, you could use the multiple-choice strategy in which students select evidence, or perhaps use sentence starters to help students formulate the beginning of their evidence. These strategies provide students with greater support as they begin the writing process.

You may decide to use the same visual representations, scaffolds, or other supports for all students, or you may want to develop individualized tools to meet the needs of specific students. Differentiating instruction includes structuring a lesson at a variety of levels in order to support an academically diverse group of students to be appropriately challenged (Adams & Pierce, 2003). Incorporating multiple modes of engagement, representation, and expression into your lessons can support all of your students in successfully engaging in scientific explanations.

Check Point

In this chapter, we described a variety of strategies to support all learners in constructing scientific explanations. We began by discussing teacher talk moves, which can serve as scaffolds, in both whole-class and small-group discussions. These strategies include teacher moves such as revoicing student ideas and asking questions that prompt students to include evidence. Utilizing a variety of talk moves can support making student thinking visible, encourage meaning making, and provide an opportunity for students to interact with and support their peers. We also described a variety of supports to help students in writing scientific explanations. These supports include writing scaffolds, visual representations, debating multiple-choice options, and checking and justifying evidence. Using a variety of different supports in your classroom can help support all students in successfully constructing scientific explanations. In the next chapter, we describe other instructional strategies for supporting students in scientific explanations. Then we continue on to discuss the design and use of assessment tasks, as well as how to create a classroom community of young scientists.

Study Group Questions

1. Videotape your class during a lesson that focuses on building scientific explanations. Watch the video and analyze the talk moves you use during instruction (see Table 4.1). What moves do you use more frequently? Less frequently? Why do you think you made those decisions?
2. Design a writing scaffold for a lesson focused on constructing scientific explanations. What was your rationale in terms of the decisions you made for the four characteristics: (a) content and general support, (b) detail and length, (c) fading, and (d) structure (see Table 4.3)?
3. Create a visual representation of the framework to display on your classroom wall. What was your rationale for the language and images that you included in the representation?

Integrating Scientific Explanation into Classroom Instruction

As a teacher, how can you engage students in generating scientific evidence that can be used to construct explanations? How can you support your students to think, talk, and write scientifically? What kinds of instructional approaches are effective with students who are engaged in this complex practice? Consider the following vignette from Mr. Meehan's second-grade classroom.

> *Mr. Meehan's second-graders were studying a unit called "Going Green in the Neighborhood." He wanted his students to investigate compost-ing, and then let the rest of the school community know the results of their study. During an initial science talk designed to help him understand what his students already knew about trash and composting, Mr. Meehan read a*

90

Integrating
Scientific
Explanation
into
Classroom
Instruction

letter from the town council about a garbage problem the community was experiencing—the landfill was getting full and there was too much garbage. He asked his students, "What can we do about all the garbage?" As his students gathered and shared their ideas and suggestions, Mr. Meehan listened to see if any students knew what happened to garbage, or if someone might suggest that some garbage will turn into soil, or if anyone was aware that some garbage could be recycled. He prompted students to identify categories of garbage. After listening to his students, the teacher found that many children knew garbage could be recycled and could list some of the materials that could be recycled. Only a few students knew the types of garbage that could turn into soil, and those students knew that food items could turn into soil; however, no students talked about paper as a possibility.

The second-graders did not use the word composting, so Mr. Meehan knew that he wanted to introduce that science term as part of his lesson. He had students save the classroom garbage for a few days, and he asked them to predict which items they thought might be able to turn into soil or compost by sorting the trash. He posted the key question for the lesson on the board: What items will turn into soil in a few weeks and which items will not compost? The students wore rubber gloves as they sorted and discussed whether trash items would compost. They recorded predictions in their science notebooks. The students worked in groups to bury selected items in large, clear plastic jars filled with soil. They drew pictures in their notebooks of how the items initially looked.

For several weeks, the class added water to their jars that they kept under heat lamps during the day. Finally, the groups dumped their jars of soil and garbage out onto news paper so they could examine the results. The students drew pictures of what they found alongside the initial pictures in their notebooks and made notes near their initial predictions. The girls and boys brought their notebooks "to The Rug" for a science talk about their observations. The class worked together to construct claims supported with evidence from the results of their investigation. They discovered, "Fruit and fruit peels will compost because we couldn't find them in our jar so we know they turned into soil. Paper towels and plates will also compost because we only found small parts of them left and we think they will soon all turn into soil. Styrofoam, plastic, and metal don't compost because we could still see them and they didn't change size." The class wrote their claims and evidence into a short newscast to share with the school during the Monday morning announcements. In this way, the student scientists made their thinking public.

In the vignette, Mr. Meehan guides his class through an investigation of composting. He carefully assesses students' prior knowledge and uses that information to make adjustments to instruction. The teacher's aim is to provide opportunities for children to collect and examine evidence in order to construct an explanation about the kinds of materials that can be composted, and share what they learn with the rest of the school. In the scenario, we see students making predictions and recording their observations in science notebooks. The focus is on explanation building, and many aspects of the investigation sequence support this process.

In this chapter, we introduce a sequence for engaging all students in productive science talks and writing with the goal of making sense of science ideas by constructing scientific explanations. The instructional sequence lays out the scientific investigation practices that are fundamental to achieving this instructional goal—asking questions, making predictions, collecting and evaluating data, constructing claims from evidence, and using scientific principles to reason about relationships between the claim and evidence. After the basic sequence has been introduced, instructional strategies for supporting students in constructing scientific explanations are provided. These supports attend to both talking and writing explanations. Video clips from elementary classrooms are used to illustrate aspects of the sequence and other instructional strategies.

Instructional Sequence for Constructing Scientific Explanations

As we discussed in the previous chapter on planning, teaching science in this way requires elementary teachers to shift from a focus on activities alone to one that involves using activities as a source of evidence from which scientific explanations can be constructed. In our work with K–5 teachers, we have learned that it is helpful to think about teaching science with an emphasis on evidence and explanation in the larger context of scientific inquiry and investigation (Zembal-Saul, 2009). This approach addresses strand 2 of proficiency in science learning (generating scientific evidence) as described in Chapter 1. The authors of *Ready, Set, Science!* characterize strand 2 as, "The knowledge and skills needed to build and refine models and explanations, design and analyze investigations, and construct and defend arguments with evidence" (Michaels et al., 2008, p. 19).

In Table 5.1, we outline the components of a basic instructional sequence for scientific investigation. Each component of the sequence will be described in more detail later in the chapter, and video clips from K–5 classrooms are included to illustrate each component. A number of video clips come from the classroom of Kimber Hershberger, one of the authors of this book. Some video from her classroom was recorded in 2009–2010 when she taught third grade; other video is from the following year in which she taught a third/fourth grade combined class. The video examples are in no way intended to imply one correct way of engaging students in the instructional sequence, but rather they have been selected to provide "images of the possible" (Hammerness et al., 2005) at different grade levels and with a variety of science content.

Before walking through each of the components of the instructional sequence, we thought it would be helpful to provide a video example from a single lesson that has many of the elements represented. This should give you a sense of how the sequence creates a context in which students explore phenomena and collect data for the purpose of constructing scientific explanations.

92

Integrating
Scientific
Explanation
into
Classroom
Instruction

TABLE 5.1 Instructional Sequence for Constructing Scientific Explanation

Sequence Component	Description
Assessing prior knowledge	Find out what students *think* they know about the big idea you will be investigating.
Framing the question	Introduce students to the question that will drive the investigation.
Making predictions	Get students to make a commitment about what they think will happen during the investigation. This can be another way of assessing prior knowledge.
Collecting, recording, and interpreting data	Provide students with an opportunity to test their predictions, collect and record data/observations, and represent and make sense of the data (e.g., create a graph, identify patterns).
Constructing a scientific explanation	Use the evidence to create a statement that answers the question (i.e., claim). Integrate reasoning to further develop the relationship between claim and evidence.

In video clip 5.1, Ms. Hershberger guides her third- and fourth-graders through a science investigation, leading the class to the point of making a scientific claim based on the evidence they collect. This lesson was conducted early in the year, so emphasis was placed on connecting evidence and claims, rather than reasoning and rebuttal. The teacher explains the procedure students will be using—attempting

VIDEO CLIP 5.1

Lesson Sequence

to move objects using the strength of compressed air in what are called "air bags" (plastic bags sealed around a straw and filled with air). She asks her students to predict four or five things that they think they will be able to lift with the air bags, and four or five things that they will not be able to lift, which they recorded on a prediction T-chart in their science notebooks. Ms. Hershberger guides the students through a general discussion of their predictions, asking them to describe the size and type of items they are identifying. The class debates as some students disagree with the predictions of their classmates. Students in the class are accustomed to disagreeing with the ideas of other students, and they do this respectfully.

When Ms. Hershberger finishes recording some of the class predictions on the board, she asks students to decide how they will record the results of their investigation. One student asks, "You mean we should have checkmarks on one side and x's on the other?" The class discusses whether this makes sense and the student realizes that he will need to test the items first before he will be able to record the results. The children begin testing items that are on the "possible to lift" side of their prediction charts, and then move on to the items that are listed on the "won't be able to lift" side. The data that they record in their notebooks will be used later as the class provides evidence for the claim that they record on the KLEW[1] chart. Students will then return to their science notebooks to write individual explanations.

Many students are excited about being able to pick up items with the air bags that they did not predict they would be able to lift. After investigating and recording what the air bags are able to lift, the class gathers in a circle on the rug to begin constructing a claim supported by their observational evidence collected during the investigation. Ms. Hershberger asks the boys and girls how they will answer the question for the day's lesson: *How strong is a bag of air?* One student answers, "It's really strong!" The teacher records the claim, *Air is really strong*, on the KLEW chart and then asks students to supply evidence to support the claim. Many students respond by sharing the heavy things they had recorded in their notebooks. In the video clip, two students share their evidence. Ms. Hershberger reminds students that the air they used is compressed in the bag, this idea is then added to the class claim on the KLEW chart: *Air is really strong when it is compressed in a bag.* The class chart contains multiple pieces of evidence to support their claim about the strength of air in a bag.

The class continues to investigate the air bags by working together to lift three people sitting on a board. Ms. Hershberger uses this lesson to help students recognize and understand some of the properties of air as an introductory investigation for a unit on "Air and Aviation." The entire investigation sequence of prediction, data collection, and discussion supports the students in being successful with the complex practice of constructing claims and evidence, and then writing scientific explanations in their individual science notebooks.

In our work with teachers, we have found it helpful to situate constructing scientific explanations within the larger context of investigation. As mentioned previously, the emphasis on activities in elementary science is well documented (Appleton, 2005; Davis, Petish, & Smithey, 2006). Given an activity-based focus, class discussion (when it occurs) tends to center on having students describe their observations and results. Rarely are observations/data seen as the jumping off point for explanation building. As we elaborate on the components of the investigation sequence in the rest of the chapter, notice how evidence is positioned. For example, the framing of the question depends on what evidence will be available for students to use to

---

[1]KLEW charts are described later in this chapter.

94

Integrating
Scientific
Explanation
into
Classroom
Instruction

construct a claim that addresses that question. In the prediction phase, students make a commitment about what they think they will observe as they investigate phenomena. During the investigation, students engage with phenomena in systematic ways, then make, record, and interpret observations/data (evidence). Through class discussion, students first share their observations/data and then use those findings as evidence to generate and support a claim(s) that addresses the guiding question. Recognizing the important role of evidence in all aspects of the investigation process facilitates teachers' development of knowledge and practices associated with constructing scientific explanations with students (Zembal-Saul, 2009).

Assessing Prior Knowledge

Contemporary perspectives on learning acknowledge that children are not "blank slates." Rather, students come to school with a rich repertoire of past experiences and prior knowledge, through which new learning is shaped (Bransford et al., 2000). Assessing students' prior knowledge in science can serve several important roles in learning and explanation building. First, assessing students' prior knowledge helps teachers uncover what students already know, as well as misunderstand, about the science ideas they will be investigating. Using this information, instruction can be adjusted to build on what students know and address limitations in their existing understanding. For example, in the opening scenario, Mr. Meehan found that many of his students knew that garbage could be recycled, but few knew that some garbage could be converted into soil. None of his students used the term *compost*. In light of this, he was able to introduce scientific terminology in context, and also shape data collection to allow students to observe the decomposition of food items and paper.

Second, by assessing the prior knowledge of the class, students become aware of the diversity of ideas that are represented within the group. Some students share similar ideas and thinking, and others bring new ideas to the table. There is value in having students listen to one another and situate their thinking within the larger range of ideas in the class.

Finally, documenting prior knowledge provides a reference point to which students can compare their developing understanding. The importance of providing opportunities for students to reflect on their thinking has been identified as an important aspect of learning; however, this is not a common practice in classrooms. We recommend having students compare and discuss the scientific explanations they develop with their initial ideas, which are documented at the beginning of a unit or sequence of lessons.

In our work with teachers of young children, we have learned that it is helpful to use materials whenever possible to elicit children's thinking and ideas. In video clip 5.2, Mrs. Kur sets up an initial sorting investigation to help her assess her students' prior knowledge and determine possible misconceptions they hold about magnets. The first-graders are asked how many of them have some prior experience with magnets—all the students eagerly raise their hands. An initial sorting investigation is introduced, and the teacher gives a bin of materials to groups of three students. The bins contain materials that are metal (both magnetic and nonmagnetic) as well as nonmetal items. Note that the students are not testing with magnets at this time; rather, they are predicting what will and will not be attracted to a magnet when they eventually do test the materials. Mrs. Kur listens as her students discuss their ideas about how to sort the materials that will be attracted to magnets from those that will not. The small groups are asked questions such as "Why are you thinking those things are magnetic? How are you making your decisions?"

Following the sorting activity, students gather for a science talk. The first-graders are instructed to share their thinking about items that will "stick" to a magnet and those that will not. As students share their thinking, Mrs. Kur asks the rest of the class if they agree or disagree with the statements. When most of the class seems to agree with a statement, the teacher writes the idea on the class chart under the heading, "What We Think We Know about Magnets." Additionally, if students have questions or items that they cannot come to agreement on, those ideas are recorded as questions under the heading, "What We Are Wondering?"

Rather than just asking her students what they think they know about magnets, Mrs. Kur

VIDEO CLIP 5.2
What We Think We Know

decided to set up an initial sorting investigation so that the students can discuss their thinking in small groups. Taking the time to look at each individual item and hearing the thinking of the other students in the group helps the first-graders clarify the ideas they have about materials that are attracted to magnets. When the students come to the whole-class meeting, they have particular points to share and everyone in the class is able to participate in the discussion of what will and will not be attracted to a magnet. As the children work on developing statements they can agree with, they also develop questions that can be answered in future investigations. Mrs. Kur has found that the approach of an initial investigation supports authentic and rich discussion about what students think they know about a topic. It provides her with opportunities to listen to the thinking of individual students and note possible misconceptions, such as "All metals are attracted to magnets." These misconceptions are recorded as questions so that she can plan specific investigations to address them throughout the unit on magnets. Mrs. Kur and her colleague have written about this approach in an article that appears in *Science & Children* (Kur & Heitzmann, 2008).

Framing the Question

In Chapter 3, we discussed the role of the question in planning for instruction for which the focus is on constructing explanations from evidence. At the most fundamental level, the question is important because the claim that is constructed as part of the scientific explanation answers the question. As you plan, you need to consider what evidence

96

Integrating
Scientific
Explanation
into
Classroom
Instruction

will actually be available to students through the investigation process, and the nature of the claim that can be developed from it. If the question is too open, students may not be able to answer it; if it is too narrow, the answer may be obvious without systematic study. For example, in the opening scenario, Mr. Meehan crafts the following question to guide instruction: *What items will turn into soil in a few weeks and which items will not compost?* The way the investigation is structured allows students to make and record observations that will provide the evidence they need to construct the claim, *Food items and paper products turn to soil, but plastic and metal do not. How does composting work?* is a seemingly small variation on the question; however, the current structure of the investigation would not yield evidence that can answer that question. The process of decomposition is not readily apparent to young students.

We mention the framing of the question again here because we have learned through our work with teachers that it is a challenging aspect of successfully integrating talking and writing scientific explanations in school science (McNeill & Knight, in review). Taking a few extra moments during the planning process to make sure the claim you intend students to construct is aligned with both the question and available data sources is well worth the effort in the long run. It is also productive to consider if you can engage students with phenomena in ways that encourage them to ask the question that guides investigation. In other words, are there new experiences you can create for students that get them wondering about what something is or why something is happening—wonderings that can be rephrased as testable questions? When students' questions drive investigation, it can be both empowering and motivating.

Throughout the description of the instructional sequence that follows, notice the ways in which teachers use the guiding question to elicit predictions, inform data collection, and orchestrate discussion aimed at explanation building.

Making Predictions

Making predictions has long been accepted as a standard feature of the investigation process in school science. Not only is it consistent with scientific practices but making predictions also can serve as a vehicle for assessing prior knowledge. We address it explicitly here for two reasons. First, when students make predictions, they commit to a position. Because making predictions frequently happens publicly as part of whole-group discussion, it provides an opportunity for students to debate ideas and explain their thinking to one another. In addition, students' predictions can serve as a jumping off point for the investigation. For instance, the teacher can encourage students to begin the data-collection phase of an investigation by testing the range of predictions shared as a class. Second, as students gain more experience with particular phenomena, they can use what they have learned to inform future predictions. This approach to making predictions is illustrated in the video clip described next, and it most closely reflects the practices of scientists.

In video clip 5.3, Ms. Hershberger's third- and fourth-grade class has begun a unit on simple machines. They are investigating the question, *How can we lift the teacher?* The children make predictions about where the brick fulcrum should be placed to help one of the smallest students in the class lift the teacher using a plank lever. The students engage in argumentation because some of them think the brick should be closer to the student and others think it should be closer to the teacher. The prediction discussion prompts one student to say, "Maybe we can try both!" The teacher responds by telling the class that they are going to do exactly that. She shows students how to build a Lego® lever with a load and adjustable fulcrum. The students are instructed to find evidence to determine where the fulcrum should be located so the student can lift the teacher.

After working in partners to test the location of the fulcrum, students gather by the plank lever and the KLEW(S) chart to make predictions based on more informed understanding from the Lego® lever investigation. Ms. Hershberger asks students to raise their hands if they think that the student will be able to lift her. Many hands shoot into the air, and the teacher asks students to place the brick fulcrum where they think it should go. One student places it close to the load. Ms. Hershberger asks the children if they agree with the location. Another student begins to express doubts about whether

VIDEO CLIP 5.3

Making Predictions

the student actually will be able to lift the teacher. She notes that she thinks it will be really hard. The teacher asks the rest of the class if they agree. Some students agree that it will be difficult, but another student suggests that based on her evidence from the Lego® experiment, she does not think it will be hard.

The prediction discussion in this case does not focus on the location of the fulcrum itself, but whether it will take a lot of effort for the small student to lift Ms. Hershberger. Despite their experiences with the Lego® lever investigation and how easily the load lifted when it was close to the fulcrum, most students are truly surprised by how easily the student lifts their teacher. Indeed, the child was able to lift Ms. Hershberger by stepping on to the board.

Taking time to thoroughly discuss and debate predictions at two different points in the lesson helps students focus on the important parts of the lever and how the location of the fulcrum changes the effort force required. As students use scientific terminology to discuss their predictions and ideas, they are able to connect those terms with concepts in context. In addition, their engagement with predicting, testing with Legos® (collecting data), and answering the question with a claim helps them write more complete scientific explanations in their notebooks.

We often get asked about the difference between a prediction and a claim. Fundamentally, we see two major differences. First, is the timing. Typically, a *prediction* is made before collecting evidence and is based on prior knowledge and

98

Integrating
Scientific
Explanation
into
Classroom
Instruction

experience. On the other hand, a claim is made after the collection of evidence, either through investigation or secondhand sources, such as researching on the Internet. The second difference is related to the role of evidence. A claim is specifically based on evidence. Consequently, engaging in predictions before an investigation can help support students in the process of explanation building, but it is different than constructing a claim based on evidence.

There is a more complex and authentic extension of using predictions. In science, what we learn from one investigation can help inform future predictions, making them more robust. This is what we begin to see in the video clip of Ms. Hershberger's class. Students make an initial prediction about whether and how the smallest student will be able to lift the teacher, and then they explore levers using Legos®. It is the results of this investigation that further inform students' predictions about lifting the teacher. Data from both the Legos® investigation and lifting the teacher ultimately contribute to the development of an evidence-based claim about the relationship between the effort force and the placement of the fulcrum and load.

Collecting, Recording, and Interpreting Data

The data-collection phase of an investigation is often very interesting and exciting to students. There is much to observe that is new, and the potential of getting sidetracked is very real. The teachers we work with have found it useful to intentionally structure their small groups to support productive investigating. For example, teachers of younger students often use the structure of "stations" because it is familiar to students from literacy instruction. When possible, an adult works at key stations to help students stay focused on the question guiding the investigation, notice important aspects of the phenomena under study, and record data onto a group chart or table. Teachers of older children often use science notebook prompts or investigation sheets to help students attend to key elements of the investigation and record data. Depending on the investigation, all small groups may be conducting the same activity so that they can pull the data and make comparisons across groups later in the lesson. In other cases, each group may be examining a different representation of the same phenomenon. This is an effective approach for comparing across representations to identify patterns.

Whatever the case, the role of the teacher during data collection is critical. Teachers have a tendency to move from group to group during an investigation, asking generic questions such as "How is it going?" or providing technical advice such as "If you hold the bottle sideways, you will have a better result." In our work we have shown that as teachers come to focus more on evidence and explanation in their science teaching, they ask questions that emphasize effective data collection and making sense of the data (Zembal-Saul, 2009). For example, teachers often ask small groups to share their observations and report on whether they see a pattern developing. They might prompt for what happens when a minor modification is made to the test, or even encourage students to begin constructing a claim from the data. Referring to the focus question frequently is useful in terms of keeping data collection and interpretation on point.

It is important to note that even young students are capable of designing a "fair test" in which they determine what to measure and how. Our purpose here is not to describe how the teacher might support this process. There are a number of excellent resources available for teachers to help students design experiments (see Harlen, 2001, and Metz, 2000). Rather, our aim is to emphasize the importance of the data-collection phase in terms of laying the groundwork for productive explanation construction. In particular, providing multiple opportunities for children to engage with the phenomenon, and the role of the teacher in getting students to identify patterns and relate the data to answering the question are essential.

VIDEO CLIP 5.4

Data Collection

To illustrate how stations can be used for students to explore different representations of the same phenomenon, we return to Mrs. Kur's first-grade class in video clip 5.4 to see how they explored the properties of solids and liquids. Mrs. Kur introduces the investigation by reminding students of a previous lesson in which they sorted water bottles filled with solids and liquids. She notes that some of the materials are ones that the students were certain about in the solid or liquid sorting. Mrs. Kur explains to her students that they are going to do four tests at different stations. The different stations are intended to give students multiple opportunities to observe and test solids and liquids under different conditions. Mrs. Kur plans to use student observations to make claims about solids and liquids, and then use those claims to make sense of the results of the tests of unknown items from their initial sort. Students work in small groups to rotate through the four different stations. All the stations have bottles partially filled with materials the class has agreed are solids or liquids. At one station the students pour the solids and liquids into plastic bowls, and they observe and discuss what happens to the items in the bowl. Another station has a balance scale, and the students are asked to make statements or predictions about the different weights of solids and liquids. At a third station students are asked to pour the materials into a clear plastic cup of water and stir the items to observe what happens to them. At the last station, students observe the materials with magnifying glasses and pour the materials into small petri dishes, so they can touch and further explore them.

As the small groups of students rotate from station to station, an adult[2] records their observations on a chart. The students openly share their thinking and observations as

---

[2]The adults who helped Mrs. Kur were parents of students and a classroom paraprofessional. The teacher writes out questions and suggestions for supporting small groups for volunteers in advance of the lesson.

100

Integrating
Scientific
Explanation
into
Classroom
Instruction

they participate in this hands-on observation of solids and liquids. When the students are asked what they observed about solids at the magnifying glass station, they reply with some of the following statements: "They have a shape" and "They can bounce." At the bowl station, the students clearly see that the liquids take the shape of the container and the solids do not. At the balance station, the students predict that liquids will be light as a feather and they are surprised that the partially filled bottle of orange juice weighs more than the partially filled bottle of blocks. At the magnifying glass/touch station, Mrs. Kur asks the students, "How do liquids feel?" The students respond, "Wet!" All of these observations are recorded on chart paper so the students have a record of their observations/data, and the charts can be used later when they discuss their claims and evidence.

After all of the groups rotate through the stations, the children gather on the carpet to share their data. Because they have multiple observations for each of the items, they are able to see patterns across the stations to help them make claims about solids and liquids. Mrs. Kur begins the science talk by reminding her students why it is important to listen to each person's statements. She asks the class, "What do you know about solids?" One student comments that solids keep their shape, and Mrs. Kur asks her to describe how she knows this. The student explains, "Teddy bears stay teddy bears." Mrs. Kur guides the student's reporting through most of the stations and asks her to support her statement that plastic teddy bears keep their shape in all of the tests she had done: They pile up in a bowl, they don't change in water, and so on. This type of data collection with multiple opportunities to interact with the materials gives the first-graders many examples and lots of data from which to identify patterns that can eventually be used to construct class claims about solids and liquids.

Constructing Scientific Explanations

Throughout this book, we have addressed the dynamic interplay of talking and writing scientific explanations (see Chapter 4). With elementary-age children, there is strong evidence that beginning with talk can be a powerful support for learning (Bransford et al., 2000; Duschl et al., 2007). More specifically, when students participate in discussions in which they co-construct claims from evidence and evaluate those claims, they are negotiating meaning of the underlying science ideas. Therefore, we recommend that with younger children, with older students who are new to the process of constructing scientific explanations, and with students who need additional support with language such as English language learners or students with special needs, whole-class discussions serve as the initial context for explanation building. Historically, discussions following science activities have been short-changed. As tempting as it may be to move on after the fun and excitement of the experimentation phase, keep in mind that the discussion is where sense making happens. All students need the opportunity to connect their observations with the associated science concepts. These connections must be forged intentionally through talk, rather than being left to chance.

101

Instructional
Sequence for
Constructing
Scientific
Explanations

Orchestrating a productive science talk is one of the most challenging classroom practices in which teachers engage. As we mentioned in Chapter 3, knowing your content storyline in advance, and in particular the explanation that you intend for students to construct, can serve as an extremely powerful tool for navigating class discussion. In addition, posting the focus question that students are attempting to answer with their explanation and keeping a bin of materials from the testing/data collection phase of the investigation sequence can support a productive discussion. We recommend beginning by having students share their data/observations. This may take some time, especially if each group experienced a different interaction with the phenomenon. In some cases, students may disagree about their observations. This is when we find it helpful to break out the materials and have a student demonstrate his or her test to the group. Inconsistencies in how materials are used to test often surface and can lead to productive talk about controlling variables in ways that result in more reliable data.

At this point, it is important to note that here is when science talks traditionally ends. The data have been shared and discussed, but not yet used as evidence to construct an explanation. Take a deep breath and press on—this is where the learning happens. After the students have shared their data/observations, it is helpful to reintroduce the question they are attempting to answer. Many interesting stories and detours tend to emerge during science talks, so using the question to set boundaries for productive talk is a useful approach. Whenever possible, having the children examine their data for patterns that can serve as the basis of a claim move the conversation forward. As students attempt to articulate appropriate claims, teacher talk moves become essential in helping the class evaluate the claims. For example, some of the talk moves you will hear often in the video clips are "Do you agree or disagree?" and "What is your evidence?" These questions encourage members of the class to consider the proposed claim and how it coordinates with the available evidence.

In video clip 5.5, Mrs. Gregg guides a kindergarten class in a science talk to construct an explanation about vibrations and sound following an investigation of three sound stations. She is the district science and math coordinator at the elementary level and a visitor in the class, which is why children are wearing name tags. The stations include using tuning forks in water, plucking the strings on a violin, and hitting a ruler on a table. The students observe the ways that three different objects produce sounds. Mrs. Gregg gathers the students on the rug in front of a chart. She has written "Claim" and "Evidence" on the chart, and under the Evidence column she

VIDEO CLIP 5.5

Claim from Evidence

102

Integrating
Scientific
Explanation
into
Classroom
Instruction

has numbered 1 through 3 so she can guide the students to use multiple pieces of evidence to support their claim. Mrs. Gregg begins by asking the students to repeat the question for the lesson: *What made the sounds?* The students respond appropriately and go on to share that they observed vibrations making the sounds at the stations. Mrs. Gregg calls on several students to describe the vibrations. The children accurately describe their observations of vibrations as the objects moving back and forth quickly. The class is then directed back to the initial question so the boys and girls can co-construct a claim. The students work with their teacher to create the claim: *All the sounds we heard were made by vibrating objects.*

Next, Mrs. Gregg asks, *"How do we know that? What did we see today that's evidence of that claim?"* She calls on one student to explain what she observed about the violin. Another student describes how the ruler makes a sound by moving his hand back and forth rapidly to demonstrate how he saw the ruler moving. Mrs. Gregg records the evidence on the chart. Finally, the class discusses the tuning forks and adds the third piece of evidence to their chart. The kindergartners are instructed to reread their evidence so they can hear it multiple times.

The three vibration stations used in this investigation provided these kindergarten children with meaningful hands-on experiences that they could use as evidence to construct a claim about the relationship between vibrations and sound. The science talk following their investigation clearly engaged these young students in the process of constructing a scientific explanation. The children were eager to share their observations and "think and act" like scientists as they discussed their understanding of how sounds are made. Listening to their peers and working together on the co-construction of a claim based on evidence helped the students solidify their understanding of the science concepts. For older children, we would go on to discuss and incorporate scientific principles into the explanation.

Instructional Strategies to Support the Explanation Building Process

As students engage in the investigation sequence and use evidence to construct scientific explanations, you can use a variety of other instructional strategies to provide further support with this practice. Instructional strategies can reinforce elements of the CER framework, or encourage students to critique explanations to further develop their understanding of the associated science ideas. Four examples of instructional strategies are provided next: (1) introducing the framework for explanation, (2) using a KLEW(S) chart, (3) critiquing a sample explanation provided by the teacher, and (4) debating an explanation provided by members of the class.

Introducing the Framework for Explanation

Research conducted by McNeill and colleagues (2006) suggests that it is important for students to be introduced explicitly to the CER framework for scientific explanation. Some of the teachers with whom we work prefer to introduce the components of the framework before they engage students in constructing explanations. Others provide students with experiences first and then introduce the terminology of the framework in context. In addition, there are multiple other approaches to introducing the framework, such as using examples from everyday life to develop definitions of claim, evidence, and reasoning. Regardless of when and how you introduce the framework, it is helpful to make a chart or other visual representation of the components and their definitions and post it in your classroom for students to refer when writing and talking science (see Chapter 4, Figure 4).

One approach to introducing the framework for scientific explanation to students is provided in Chapter 2 (video clip 2.1). Recall that Ms. Hershberger prefers first to engage her students in science investigations in which they became familiar with drawing conclusions from data so that when she formally introduces the components of the CER framework, the children can easily reconnect to their prior experiences. Through whole-class discussion, the teacher reviews the components of scientific explanation with students and supports them in constructing working definitions for each component. Ms. Hershberger then creates a poster using students' language for explanation, which is displayed in the classroom for the rest of the year and used by the class as a reference when talking and writing explanations.

Another way to introduce the framework for scientific explanation is by using relevant examples from everyday life. In the following example, Mrs. Grube assists her fifth-grade students in understanding the parts of a scientific explanation using an example based on a popular singer at the time, Justin Bieber.

First, Mrs. Grube played a YouTube video of the hit song, "Baby." Then she wrote the following claim on the board: "Justin Bieber is the best musician that ever lived." Her class reacted strongly to the claim, saying things like: "What about Beethoven?" and "That's your opinion!" Mrs. Grube asked her class to think about her claim and explain why it was a claim. One student responded that a claim is a statement, and, when prompted by Mrs. Grube, added that it's a statement that answers some problem or question in science. The teacher clarified that in this case they were not answering a science question, but were looking at the Justin Bieber claim as a way of understanding the parts of a scientific explanation. When they were asked to think about the question her claim responded to, student proposed, "Who is the best musician in the world?"

Mrs. Grube continued the discussion by asking, "What would I need to show you to make my claim more valid?" A student suggested that the teacher should use observations and data that support the claim. Another student offered the word *evidence* and Mrs. Grube wrote: "Evidence uses observations and data to back up a claim." Next, Mrs. Grube supplied some specific evidence to support her claim about Justin Bieber. She listed that his YouTube videos have millions of hits and that

104

Integrating
Scientific
Explanation
into
Classroom
Instruction

he won twenty-two music awards in 2009. The class discussed the merits of the evidence and one student gave a convincing argument that just because people watch his videos doesn't mean they like him; maybe they watch them to make fun of him. The second piece of evidence about his awards was considered "good" evidence.

Finally, Mrs. Grube introduced the idea of scientific reasoning as a way to explain why the evidence supports the claim. The students decided that winning awards is one way to say that someone is the best. Mrs. Grube added the statement: "Winning awards means that someone is the best, and since Justin Bieber won twenty-two music awards, you can claim that he is the best." However, one student continued to argue with Mrs. Grube's initial claim that he was the best musician who ever lived. He felt that she didn't have evidence to support that he was the best in all categories, such as classical or country. Another student added that winning the awards in 2009 didn't make him the best musician that ever lived in any time period. Mrs. Grube used their arguments to introduce the term *science discourse* and stated that differences of opinion help us make better claims and encourage us to examine our evidence. She changed her initial claim to read: "Justin Bieber is the most popular pop musician of 2009." Not all of the students were willing to agree with her, but they at least felt her claim was stated more accurately given the supporting evidence.

KLEW(S) Chart

Mapping an explanation over time as claims are constructed from evidence can be a powerful instructional tool for both students and teachers. For students, documenting claims and their direct connection to evidence and reasoning across a unit can help them make connections among science ideas. For the teacher, creating an explanation map for a unit can begin during instructional planning and serve as a way to negotiate the content terrain while teaching the unit, keeping the coherent content storyline at the forefront (Zembal-Saul, 2009). In our work, we have modified a well-known reading comprehension strategy called the KWL (Ogle, 1986) for the purpose of teaching science. In the original version, students document what they know (K), want (W) to know, and have learned (L) from a text.

In the science version of the KLEW chart, emphasis is placed on connecting claims and evidence (see Table 5.2). The K column is used to document assessment of prior knowledge and is framed as WHAT WE *THINK* WE **KNOW**. This allows for initial thinking, whether or not it is scientifically accurate, to be recorded prior to investigation and explanation building. We have found it useful to use this aspect of the chart as a vehicle for reflecting on learning over time as students develop deeper understanding of the science. In the second column of the KLEW chart, we describe WHAT ARE WE **LEARNING**? This is where claims are recorded throughout a unit as they are generated, usually following each series of investigations. Even though this is the second column of the chart, it is not necessarily the second step in the instructional sequence. Students first collect, record, and discuss data[3] from

---

[3]Note that we actually do not consider data to be evidence as such until it is used in connection with a claim, but we do not make this distinction with children.

105

Instructional
Strategies to
Support the
Explanation
Building
Process

TABLE 5.2 KLEW Chart Components

Compon ent	Description
KNOW (K)	Document the assessment of prior knowledge by asking, "What do you *think* you know about _____?"
LEARNING (L)	This is the claim column, based on statements of learning in response to the guiding question.
EVIDENCE (E)	Evidence is added to the chart when students share their observations before claims are constructed. Arrows are used on the chart to connect claims to multiple pieces of evidence.
WONDERINGS (W)	Testable questions are documented as they arise and every effort is made to test them at some point in the unit. Testable questions often surface during investigation. Misconceptions can be rephrased as testable questions.
SCIENTIFIC PRINCIPLES (S)	Throughout the unit, science concepts are added to this column. They are used during discussion to build a more complete explanation by further elaborating the connection among claims and evidence.

their investigations, which is documented in the next column, WHAT'S YOUR **EVIDENCE**? In practice, we have found it helpful to directly connect claims in the *L* column to particular supporting evidence in the *E* column using arrows. The final column is for **WONDERINGS** and can be used throughout the instructional sequence to record students' questions that arise during investigation and other aspects of science instruction, especially those that are testable questions and can be revisited and pursued as part of another lesson. In addition, many of the teachers that we work with rephrase misconceptions as wonderings so as not to place students on the spot.

Since we initially published our article on using KLEW charts in science instruction (Hershberger, Zembal-Saul, & Starr, 2006), we added another column for **SCIENTIFIC** PRINCIPLES, making it a KLEW(S) chart. The new column addresses the importance of reasoning and the need to draw on science concepts when developing the relationship among claims and evidence. We often have students refer to resources, such as reference books or science sites on the Internet, to generate a list of Scientific Principles that they can use for reasoning when constructing explanations.

A sample KLEW(S) chart that was developed by a third-grade class during a unit on simple machines is shown in Figure 5.1 (see also video clip 5.7 later in the chapter). Note that it includes scientific principles (S). KLEW charts also can be adapted for use with younger children or students who need additional support with language. For example, one teacher uses images to prompt students' recollection of the focus

106

Integrating
Scientific
Explanation
into
Classroom
Instruction

FIGURE 5.1

KLEWS Chart Developed by Third-Grade Class for Simple Machines

of each of the columns—a brain for what we think we know; a light bulb for what are we learning; eyes for what is our evidence; and a question mark for wonderings. In addition to adapting KLEW charts for use with different grade levels and students with different backgrounds, the structure can also be used to support scientific writing in addition to class discussion. Following a science talk in which students construct an explanation, we recommend that older students attempt to write the claims, evidence, and reasoning in their own words in their science notebooks.

In video clip 5.6, we see a KLEW(S) chart used to support explanation building. Ms. Hershberger's third- and fourth-grade class is working on an investigation of conductors and insulators as part of an electricity unit. Prior to this lesson, students had worked in groups to predict, sort, and test a bin of materials. The students recorded the results in their science notebooks, and the teacher added the results to a class data chart. The chart had columns for listing the items, the material, predictions, and results. As the clip begins, we hear Ms. Hershberger ask students if they can see any patterns in the data to answer the question, *Which materials will allow the electric current to flow?* The students notice that all the metal materials allow the current to flow. The teacher uses a red marker to highlight the pattern in materials and results. She asks students to state the evidence they found to answer the focus question. One child provides a detailed description that metals made the light bulb work, which the teacher records as evidence on the class KLEW(S) chart.

After rereading the key question, Ms. Hershberger asks students to make a claim that answers the question. One student states, "Metal materials help the electric current to flow." Next, the teacher redirects the class to look again at their data chart to identify patterns to answer the second part of the question, *Which materials don't allow the electrical current to flow?* The class notes the types of materials that had a "no" in the results column, and Ms. Hershberger adds additional evidence to the KLEW(S) chart. "Paper, plastic, wood, metal oxide, and glass didn't allow the electric current to flow so the bulb didn't light." One student requests that the word *insulators* be added to the evidence statement.

VIDEO CLIP 5.6
Looking for Patterns

Next, Ms. Hershberger points to the S column of the KLEW(S) chart where she had a list of words and principles related to electricity. She tells the class that she wants them to think about what was going on with the atoms of materials that are conductors and insulators. One student suggests that the atoms of insulators were more stable than those of conductors. The teacher reads about insulators from an informational book about electricity, and the students find that their ideas about what is going on with atoms is scientifically correct. The new science principles are added to the KLEW(S) chart. Ms. Hershberger added: "Insulators are materials that hold their electrons tightly so they don't move from atom to atom and this stops the flow of electrical current. Conductors are materials that don't hold their electrons tightly so they can move from atom to atom causing an electrical current and completing the circuit."

Following the discussion of the data and the addition of evidence, claims, and scientific principles to the KLEW(S) chart, students wrote scientific explanations in their energy and electricity notebooks (see Figure 5.2). Each student was given Post-its® with the words *claim, evidence,* and *reasoning* on them so the Post-its® could be "stuck" on the notebook pages about conductors and insulators to show that all parts of a scientific explanation were included. Students used the statements from the S part of the KLEW(S) chart to add reasoning by writing about the electrons in conductors and insulators. For example, one student wrote: "When conductors complete the circuit the electrons flow and the light turns on, but when there is an insulator the electrons don't flow and circuit is incomplete. Insulators do not allow electrical current to flow so the light turns off." As students used the Post-its® to mark the parts of the explanation, some students realized that they were missing one of the parts of the explanation and then revised their notebook entry to include it.

108

Integrating
Scientific
Explanation
into
Classroom
Instruction

FIGURE 5.2

Sample Science Notebook Page with CER Marked with Post-its®

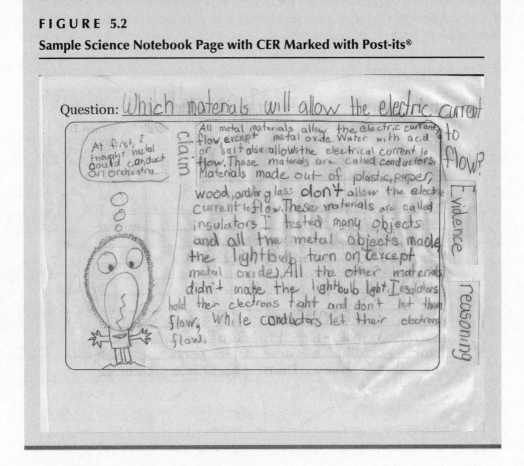

Critique a Sample Explanation

Discussing and critiquing sample explanations can provide students with models of strong and weak scientific explanations. This can be a valuable instructional strategy to help students develop a stronger understanding of what counts as strong claims, evidence, and reasoning. Furthermore, you can purposefully design examples that include common student difficulties with the different components. For example, if students are struggling with including specific measurements and details in the evidence, one sample could include this weakness in order to encourage a class discussion on how to improve the evidence.

In video clip 5.7, Ms. Hershberger's class is about to investigate pulleys as part of their simple machines unit. Before they begin the investigations, she wants them to add a claim and evidence for inclined planes to the KLEW chart. At the beginning of the clip, the teacher reviews the parts of an explanation with the class. One student identifies claims, evidence, and scientific principles. Ms. Hershberger points out the chart posted in the classroom that they developed during a previous lesson. She states, "The claim answers the question based on evidence." Next, Ms. Hershberger explains to the class that she has developed three different claims that she wants them to review and decide which one they should put on the KLEW chart. She posts them on the board for students to examine, and marks them A, B, and C. After a few minutes, students share their responses. Ms. Hershberger asks one student to explain why he selected A. He reads claims A and B and points out that Claim B does not say anything about distance—he exclaims, "Distance is very important." The teacher asks another student to share his thinking and whether he agrees or disagrees. This student focuses on Claim C, pointing out the false information that it includes. He explains that an inclined plane decreases the amount of effort force by increasing the distance across which it is moved, as opposed to the other way around. Ms. Hershberger asks, "And how do you know that?" The student refers to all of the experiments the class has done which demonstrate the same idea.

VIDEO CLIP 5.7
Critique Teacher Example

A few more students share their thinking, and one girl agrees that distance is important. Another student restates the force and distance relationship, and the teacher gently presses her to explain her thinking. The student refers to their investigations of levers for which they uncovered the same force and distance relationship. Ms. Hershberger compliments students for noticing patterns across the simple machines. Given the strong support for Claim A, she moves it into the *L* column of the KLEW chart and asks the students what else they need to add to the chart to build their explanation. One child responds, "Evidence." Once again, the teacher shares samples with the class that she prepared in advance. Students examine the evidence summaries, and are asked to share their selections using sign language.

Although the clip ends here, you can get a sense of how effective it can be for students to critique examples of claims and evidence provided by the teacher. By asking whether students agree or disagree with one another, and by prompting them to explain their thinking, all students have access to important science ideas and how their peers think about them. Not only does this approach help model how to evaluate components of the framework but students also participate in productive critique, helping to establish a well-functioning learning community.

Debate a Peer Explanation

Debating a peer explanation includes having students share their scientific explanations with the class, critique the different components of the explanations, and come to a consensus as a class on what should be included in the strongest explanation.

110

Integrating
Scientific
Explanation
into
Classroom
Instruction

Engaging in this process can support students in improving the quality of their own scientific explanations. Furthermore, it encourages students to listen to each other's ideas as well as work together as a community in order to come to agreement.

Video clip 5.8 shows Ms. Hershberger's third-grade students working in small groups to collect data about different types of pulleys using force meters. Following the investigation, the children worked in their groups to write claims and evidence based on their data. As the class gathers for a science talk, the students are asked to critique the claims and evidence written by others. The video begins with Mason sharing his group's claim about combining a fixed pulley and a moveable pulley. He reads from his journal page, "The fixed/moveable pulley helps us to do work by decreasing the amount of force and changing the direction of the pull." Baron critiques the claim by reading an alternative one written by his group, which includes the idea that more distance is involved. Baron explains that he thinks it is important to include the amount the rope that was pulled to move the load. Allison adds to the conversation by reading the claim that her group constructed, which included the comparison between a straight lift and the pulley. She argues that it is important to state what is being increased and decreased. Joe notes that the first group did not include distance and his group did not include the straight lift, so the class decides to use the claim written by the third group on the KLEW(S) chart.

VIDEO CLIP 5.8
Critiquing Peer Explanation

Ms. Hershberger continues the science talk by asking students to share their evidence. Kayla reads the evidence used by her group, which included the materials they used to collect data, but another student notes this group did not include any specific data. Ms. Hershberger asks for specific data that students have and Mason begins by reading a data statement from his paper and then provides a verbal description of data from the chart on his recording sheet. It is clear that the evidence he cites is not written on his paper, but he is able to articulate the significance of the data he provides. Baron adds to what Mason has shared by saying that he thinks the evidence needs to include the exact distance of the pull.

This investigation occurred near the end of a unit on simple machines in which the lessons were intentionally scaffolded so that students could draw on their prior experiences to write claims and evidence independently or in small groups. The students were comfortable with listening for specific information provided in the claim and also listening for specific data points that were shared as evidence. Working in small groups to co-construct the claims and evidence encouraged the students to think through all the information and attempt to include more specific details in their writing. Following the sharing, Ms. Hershberger recorded the group's explanation on the KLEW(S) chart while students returned to their seats to add more specific details to their individual explanations.

The four instructional strategies we discussed in this section—introducing the framework for explanation, using a KLEW(S) chart, critiquing a sample explanation provided by the teacher, and debating an explanation provided by members of the class—are all tools that you can use to further reinforce the explanation building process. By using a variety of scaffolds and strategies in your instruction, you incorporate different avenues to support all learners in this valuable process.

Check Point

During the previous chapters, we discussed the importance of engaging in scientific explanation, the role of the CER framework, a process to identify and design appropriate opportunities in the science curriculum for scientific explanation and different types of supports for scientific talk and writing. In this chapter, we described a variety of other strategies you can integrate into your instruction to assist all learners in constructing explanations. We began by describing an instructional sequence that can help students engage in constructing scientific explanations: (1) assessing prior knowledge; (2) framing the question; (3) making predictions; (4) collecting, recording, and interpreting data; and (5) constructing a scientific explanation. Next, we described a variety of instructional strategies to support student learning, including introducing the CER framework, using a KLEW(S) chart, critiquing a teacher explanation, and debating a peer explanation. A teacher would never use all of these strategies in one lesson. Rather, we view these strategies as part of a toolkit that you can draw from in order to support all the students in your class in justifying the claims they make in both talk and writing. In the next chapter, we will focus on using the CER framework to design assessments and rubrics to evaluate student learning, provide constructive feedback, and modify instruction to better meet the needs of all students.

Study Group Questions

1. Design a science lesson that includes the five components of the instructional sequence (see Table 5.1). How is this similar to and different from science lessons you have designed in the past? How might this lesson support students in constructing scientific explanations?

2. Incorporate either critiquing a teacher explanation or debating a peer explanation into a lesson. What strengths and weaknesses did the students notice about the claims, evidence, and reasoning?

3. Build a KLEW(S) chart with your students (see Table 5.2). How did the explanation the class constructed change over time? What aspects were easier for them and what aspects were more challenging?

Designing Assessment Tasks and Rubrics

How can you design assessments to evaluate your students' abilities to construct scientific explanations? How can you use the data from the assessments to inform your own instruction? Consider the following vignette from Mr. Garcia's first-grade classroom.

Mr. Garcia is finishing up a unit on magnets with his first-grade students. During the unit, he focused on the key science concepts in the following content standard:

Magnets attract and repel each other and certain kinds of other materials. (NRC, 1996, B:1/4, K-4)

Furthermore, he emphasized supporting his students in using evidence from the investigations they completed in class to construct and evaluate claims:

Use data to construct a reasonable explanation.
(NRC, 1996, A:1/4, K-4)

Mr. Garcia wants to evaluate his first-grade students' understandings of these two important science standards. Furthermore, he wants the students to review the investigations they have done as well as review all the claims and evidence that they have recorded as a class throughout the unit. Mr. Garcia just returned from the annual meeting of the National Science Teachers Association, which gave him an idea. He decides to do an assessment through a science conference, which will allow him to assess his students' understanding from the unit and give them a chance to share science in a community like scientists do in the real world. The next morning, he introduces the end of the unit assessment to his students.

Mr. Garcia: Good morning, first-graders. I just came back from a science conference. What do you think I did there?

Sam: Did lots of experiments?

Olivia: Wore your lab coat?

Mr. Garcia: Actually, most of the time I sat and listened to other science teachers talk about what they were learning and doing. We are almost finished with our unit on magnets and I thought that it would be a good idea for us to have our own science conference. I want you to work with a partner and wear your lab coats and pick one claim from our magnet chart to explain and demonstrate what you know about magnets.

Marcel: Do we get to use lots of real magnets and stuff?

Mr. Garcia: Certainly, the most interesting workshops I went to were ones where the scientists had real stuff for us to see.

Juanita: I want to do the magnetic field.

Jake: Me, too! That was so cool!

Lin: I want to make the doughnuts dance.

Mr. Garcia: What would your claim be?

Lin: That . . . that magnets can attract and repel each other.

Mr. Garcia: What is your evidence to support that claim?

Lin: That we made the doughnuts magnets repel each other so they danced on a pencil.

Mr. Garcia: Do you remember any other things that would support the claim that magnets attract and repel?

Lin: Ummmm.

Kris: The mystery envelopes!

Mr. Garcia: Let's read over our claims chart together and decide which students would like to write a script for each of the claims.

(The class decides who will work on each claim and Mr. Garcia writes their names on Post-its® and puts them beside the claims on the chart.)

Mr. Garcia: What do you think we should include in our scripts?

Olivia: The stuff we need to use to show what we did.

Mr. Garcia: Yes, you can make a list of materials. What else should we write on the script?

Sam: Maybe like an introduction kind of thing like: Ladies and Gentlemen!

Mr. Garcia: You could put that in, but since this is a science conference what do you think scientists might include?

Marcel: Evidence. We need evidence so people will know how we know things.

Claudia: Yeah, scientists have data so people will believe them— like we got data for which magnet was strongest. I am going to do that one.

Mr. Garcia: Sounds like lots of you have good ideas for the conference. I'm going to give you a paper so you and your partner can list the materials you need, write who is going to say the claim and who is going to share the evidence. You should think of two or three demonstrations as evidence for what you are claiming.

This vignette illustrates how a teacher can design an assessment that targets key science concepts *and* scientific explanations to assess student learning of both of these essential learning goals. Through careful design, assessments can be developed to make student thinking visible either through science talk, as in this case, or through science writing. In this chapter, we discuss five steps that can be used to develop either written or oral scientific explanation assessment tasks. These steps include the development of a specific rubric, which can be a valuable tool to provide students with feedback on their work. We will use two different examples to illustrate what these steps look like in practice in both talk and writing. Finally, we will discuss how the claim, evidence, and reasoning framework can also be used to assess student understanding in more informal science talks, which can be particularly beneficial for the early elementary grades.

Overview of the Development Process

Assessment is a key component of classroom instruction for a variety of reasons. Often assessments are discussed in terms of both formative and summative assessments. Engaging students in scientific explanation can serve both of these roles. *Formative assessments* are measures that help make students' thinking visible so that teachers can use that information to inform and modify their instruction (NRC, 2001). Having students construct scientific explanations in either talk or writing provides you with insight into how students are making sense of the data they have collected in terms of the claims they make and how they justify those claims. *Summative assessments* provide a measure of students' performance relative to a specific target typically at the end of a unit or after a topic has been covered (NRC, 2001). Scientific explanations can serve as an important summative tool to evaluate whether students have achieved your learning goals in terms of both developing a stronger understanding of the science content and scientific explanations.

In this chapter, we describe our development process for designing scientific explanation assessment tasks, as well as how data from those assessments can inform instruction. Our process consists of five steps (see Table 6.1). We first identify and unpack the target content standard with which we want the assessment to align. Then we determine the level of complexity of the scientific explanation task, such as if we want students to use multiple pieces of evidence or include reasoning. Next, we create a learning performance that specifically combines the science content and the claim, evidence, and reasoning framework. Finally, we write the assessment task and develop a rubric that clarifies our expectations for the different components of the scientific explanation. We will use two examples to illustrate each of these steps in more detail. One example is from a fourth-grade classroom that constructed written scientific explanations about force and motion. The second example is from a third-grade classroom that created podcasts about electricity and circuits. We selected these two examples to illustrate that scientific explanations can be assessed through a more traditional paper-and-pencil test, but they also can be assessed through science talk in different projects. Using a variety of ways to assess student learning can provide you with a more accurate measure of your students' level of understanding, particularly for English language learners who may struggle to express their science knowledge in a traditional written test (Olson et al., 2009).

TABLE 6.1 Development Process for Scientific Explanation Assessment Tasks

Step 1: Identify and unpack the content standards.

Step 2: Select scientific explanation level of complexity.

Step 3: Create learning performance.

Step 4: Write the assessment task.

Step 5: Develop specific rubric.

Step 1: Identify and Unpack the Content Standard

The first step in the process of developing science assessments is to identify a science standard that aligns with the goals of your instruction and to unpack the key science concepts in the standard. The standard can be a national standard, state standard, or district standard depending on the policies of your particular school. Aligning the assessment with the standard encourages you to consider how the assessment and related instruction address the content in these documents.

Furthermore, this step encourages you to think deeply about the science goal. The unpacking process includes two components: (1) considering the science ideas in the standard and (2) identifying any common student alternative conceptions related to the standard. As we mentioned in Chapter 3, a science learning goal is not just a topic, like *seeds*. Rather, a learning goal goes more in depth, like: *A seed is the part of a plant that contains the baby plant (embryo) with its protective coat and stored food that can develop into a new plant under proper conditions*. This learning goal describes in more depth the science ideas related to seeds that are important for elementary students to understand.

The other component is identifying any common student alternative conceptions related to the standard. As part of students' experiences in their everyday lives, they develop ideas about the natural world that may not align with the scientifically accepted ones (Driver, Guesne, & Tiberghien, 1985). Consequently, these student ideas' are often referred to as *alternative conceptions* or *misconceptions*, because they are not scientifically accurate. For example, students may think that any small object is a seed (e.g., a button) or any small food object is a seed (e.g., a piece of pasta). When designing assessments, we want to know if students still hold these alternative conceptions or not. Acquiring this information can be essential for providing students with feedback and informing future instruction. Consequently, at times we purposefully incorporate alternative conceptions in our design of assessment tasks.

Fourth-Grade Writing Case: Unpacking

The first example comes from a fourth-grade classroom that was in the middle of a science unit studying force and motion using the Science and Technology for Children (STC) Motion and Design unit (NSRC, 2003). Ms. Robinson decided to develop a writing prompt as a formative assessment to go along with a scientific investigation focused on how the size of the force impacts the motion of a vehicle. She was interested in assessing her students' understanding of the force and motion concepts, as well as their ability to justify their claims with appropriate evidence and reasoning. Specifically, the investigation aligned with the first half of the content standard in Table 6.2 from the *Benchmarks for Science Literacy* (AAAS, 2009): *The*

TABLE 6.2 Unpacking of Force and Motion Standard

Standards	Clarifying the Standard	Student Alternative Conceptions
The greater the force is, the greater the change in motion will be. The more massive an object is, the less effect a given force will have (AAAS, 2009, 4F/E1bc).	• A force is a push or a pull. • A greater force is a larger push or a larger pull. • A larger force will cause a greater change in the motion of an object such as making an object move faster, move slower or change direction.	• Students think force is a property of the object and is not influenced by the size of the push or the pull (Driver, Squires, Rushworth & Wood-Robinson, 1994). • Students think motion exists in only two categories—moving and not moving—rather than considering the speed of an object (Driver et al., 1994).

greater the force is, the greater the change in motion will be. Consequently, the clarification of the standard in Table 6.2 focuses on the first half of the standard (in italics).

In order to understand the first half of this standard, students need to know that a force is a push or a pull, a greater force is a larger push or pull, and a larger force will cause a greater change in the motion of an object such as making an object move faster, move slower, or change direction. These ideas can be challenging for students, because they generally think of force as a property of an object (e.g., a car has a force) rather than think of a force as a push or a pull (e.g., when my hand pushes the car, it applies a force) (Driver et al., 1994). Another common alternative conception is that students think of objects as moving or not moving and do not consider the speed of an object (Driver et al., 1994). Ms. Robinson wanted her students to collect data and write a scientific explanation that demonstrated that they understood that the size of the force is proportional to the change in speed of the vehicle.

Third-Grade Podcast Case: Unpacking

The second example comes from a third-grade classroom that was finishing a unit on energy and electricity. As a summative assessment for the unit, Ms. Sasaki decided to have her students develop podcasts. She believed that the podcasts would be an excellent way for the students to review and explain what they had learned during the unit. By using this creative venue, she was able to encourage some students who typically struggled in science to make their thinking visible and engage in discourse about science concepts. Specifically, her goal was to have students share claims about energy and electricity supported by evidence from investigations they had completed in class. The assessment she designed aligned with the electricity standard from the *National Science Education Standards* (NRC, 1996) displayed in Table 6.3: *Electrical circuits require a complete loop through which an electrical current can pass*. Specifically, she focused on the parts of the standard that talk about making light bulbs light and complete circuits (in italics) so the clarification focuses on those aspects of the standard.

TABLE 6.3 Unpacking the electricity standard

Standards	Clarifying the Standard	Student Alternative Conceptions
Electricity in circuits can produce light, heat, sound, and magnetic effects. Electrical circuits require a complete loop through which an electrical current can pass (NRC, 1996, B:1/3, K-4).	• Electricity is a form of energy that can produce light. • A circuit is a path that electricity can flow or move through. The path is made out of materials that allow the movement of electricity (e.g., metal). There are some materials that do not allow the movement of electricity (e.g., rubber). • In order for a circuit to produce light (e.g., light a light bulb), the path has to be a complete loop or complete circle for the electricity to flow through. If there is a gap in the loop or a material in the loop that does not allow the movement of electricity (e.g., rubber), it is not a complete circuit. Without a complete circuit, the light bulb will not light up.	• Students think that a light bulb just needs to be connected to a battery to light. There needs to be a linear path from the battery to the light bulb, but not a complete loop or circle (Grotzer & Perkins, 2005). • Students think that materials that are actually insulators can allow electricity to move through them (e.g., rubber) or they can be confused about what is inside some objects (e.g., light bulb).

Ms. Sasaki wanted her students to develop an understanding of complete circuits, that a circuit is a path that electricity can flow or move through and that in order for a circuit to be complete, it needs to include an unbroken circle or loop. She knew that some students struggled with this idea and so she began the unit with the alternative conception that a light bulb just needed to be connected to a battery in a linear pathway (not a circle) in order to light (Grotzer & Perkins, 2005). Consequently, Ms. Sasaki hoped her students would be able to provide evidence in their podcasts for the claim that a complete circuit was necessary to light a light bulb.

Step 2: Select Scientific Explanation Level of Complexity

In Chapter 2, we introduced multiple variations of the scientific explanation framework, which can be used depending on your students' level of experience and comfort level with constructing scientific explanations. When designing a scientific explanation assessment item, it is important to consider what variation you want your students to include in their responses. Table 6.4 provides a summary of the different variations that we previously discussed.

Variation #1 includes a focus on the first two components of the framework, claim and evidence, and the idea that students should be justifying their claims with evidence. Variation #2 becomes more complex in its discussion of evidence and encouraging students to include more than one piece of evidence to support their claim. In Variation #3, reasoning is also included in that students are expected to

TABLE 6.4 Summary of Four Different Variations of the Scientific Explanation Framework

Variation	Description of Framework
Variation #1	1. Claim 2. Evidence
Variation #2	1. Claim 2. Evidence • Multiple pieces
Variation #3	1. Claim 2. Evidence • Multiple pieces 3. Reasoning
Variation #4	1. Claim 2. Evidence • Multiple pieces 3. Reasoning 4. Rebuttal

explain how or why their evidence supports their claim using appropriate science ideas. Finally, Variation #4 also includes a rebuttal in that students are also expected to discuss alternative claims and to provide additional evidence and/or reasoning for why the alternative is not appropriate. Considering which variation serves as your learning goal for your students can help you in designing an optimal question that gives them the opportunity and support to provide those components.

In addition to considering the variation of the scientific explanation framework to use, it can also be beneficial to consider any challenges your students are having with the framework. For example, if your students are struggling to include multiple pieces of evidence in their scientific explanations, you may want to explicitly design either the question or the supports to encourage them to consider more than one piece of evidence.

Fourth-Grade Writing Case: Level of Complexity

For Ms. Robinson's class, her expectation was that her students justify the claims they made with both evidence and reasoning. Consequently, the focus of the assessment item was on Variation #3, which includes (1) claim, (2) evidence—multiple pieces, and (3) reasoning. Over the course of the school year, Ms. Robinson's students struggled with including reasoning in their scientific explanations. Consequently, she focused her instruction on supporting her students to include science ideas and scientific language in their reasoning as they explained why their evidence supported their claim. In the development of the motion assessment item, she wanted her students to be using the scientific idea that the greater the force, the greater the change in motion of the object as they made sense of the data they collected in their motion experiment.

Third-Grade Podcast Case: Level of Complexity

In Ms. Sasaki's class, she focused on Variation #2 of the framework, because her students were new at constructing scientific explanations. She wanted her students to focus on constructing claims using evidence from the investigations they had completed in class as well as their data charts in their science notebooks. Ms. Sasaki also wanted her students to become comfortable with claims and evidence before she included a specific focus on articulating their reasoning for why their evidence supported their claim. However, she did want her third-graders to include multiple pieces of evidence to support their claims, which is why she focused on Variation #2 over Variation #1. In their podcasts, she hoped students would make claims about electrical circuits and justify those claims using evidence from the investigations that they had conducted.

Step 3: Create Learning Performances

After unpacking the science content and selecting the target variation of the scientific explanation framework, the next step is to create the learning performance. As we discussed in Chapter 3, developing learning performances are an important step in planning for instruction, because they encourage you to articulate the learning goal specifically in terms of how students will need to apply their science knowledge in a particular context. Learning performances combine both the science content and the scientific inquiry practice to explicitly articulate what the application or use of the content knowledge will look like for students (Krajcik et al., 2008). In this book, we specifically focus on the scientific inquiry practice of constructing scientific explanations. Consequently, the development of the learning performance combines the science content knowledge with the variation of the framework you have selected for your students. This allows you to articulate an explicit learning goal that can guide both your development of the assessment task and the associated rubric.

Fourth-Grade Writing Case: Learning Performance

The science content in Ms. Robinson's class focused on the idea that the greater the force on the object, the greater the change in motion of that object will be (e.g., travel farther or faster). Yet the goal was not for the fourth-graders just to define this science idea, but rather they should apply the concept to make sense of their force and motion investigations. Figure 6.1 illustrates how the science content was combined with Variation #3 of the framework (i.e., claim, evidence, and reasoning) to develop a specific learning performance that articulates the learning goal for the students.

The learning performance specifies that the assessment should allow students the opportunity to (1) make a claim about the motion of an object; (2) provide evidence to support that claim in terms of data, including both the size of the force

FIGURE 6.1

Force and Motion Learning Performance

Content Standard ×	Scientific Explanation = (Scientific Inquiry Standard)	Learning Performance
The greater the force is, the greater the change in motion will be. The more massive an object is, the less effect a given force will have (AAAS, 2009, 4F/E1bc).	Use data to construct a reasonable explanation (NRC, 1996, A: 1/4, K-4). Communicate investigations and explanations (NRC, 1996, A: 1/5, K-4).	Students construct a scientific explanation stating a claim about the motion of an object, providing evidence in the form of data about the force applied to an object and the motion of the object (e.g., distance traveled, speed, or direction), and reasoning about the greater the force is, the greater the change in motion will be.

and the change in motion of the object; and finally, (3) supply reasoning that clearly uses the science idea to explain why the evidence supports the claim. The learning performance provides an explicit goal for the students' writing.

Third-Grade Podcast Case: Learning Performance

The third-grade students were at the end of the unit focused on energy and electricity. In terms of the electrical circuit podcast, Ms. Sasaki's goal was for the students to make claims about what they had learned was needed in a circuit for a light bulb to light up and to provide evidence for those claims. She did not want her students simply to define the concepts they had learned about (i.e., like the definition of a closed circuit). Rather, she wanted her students to use the observations and data they had collected in their investigations as part of their podcasts to prove to the audience why various components and characteristics are important in an electrical circuit. Figure 6.2 illustrates a learning performance for this goal. The learning performance combines the science content in the electrical circuit standard with Variation #2 of the scientific explanation framework, which includes a focus on claims and evidence.

The learning performance illustrates specifically what students should be able to do in their podcasts in terms of demonstrating what they have learned about circuits and their ability to use evidence to support claims.

Step 4: Write the Assessment Task

The three previous steps provide clear guidelines for the development of the assessment task, which can serve as either a formative or a summative assessment of student learning. Unpacking the content standard encourages you to think about

FIGURE 6.2
Electrical Circuit Learning Performance

Content Standard ×	Scientific Explanation = (Scientific Inquiry Standard)	Learning Performance
Electricity in circuits can produce light, heat, sound, and magnetic effects. Electrical circuits require a complete loop through which an electrical current can pass. (NRC, 1996, B:1/3, K-4).	Use data to construct a reasonable explanation (NRC, 1996, A: 1/4, K-4).

Communicate investigations and explanations (NRC, 1996, A: 1/5, K-4). | Students construct scientific explanations stating a claim about what is required to make a circuit that produces light (e.g., a complete loop) and evidence in the form of observations from their investigations about what materials and configuration of materials allowed the light bulb to light. |

the key science concepts that you want to target in the assessment. Selecting the variation of the framework helps you to consider your expectations for the students in terms of what they should be including in their scientific explanations. Finally, developing the learning performance combines the content and scientific explanation learning goals to define explicitly what you hope to see in either the students' writing or science talks. These steps can help provide guidance in the actual development of the assessment task. In addition, the development of the assessment task also requires considering the actual context in which students will be constructing their scientific explanations in talk or writing.

For the context, you want students to be constructing scientific explanations around a specific phenomenon or investigation (e.g., the motion of a toy car) and not just about the science concept in general (e.g., forces make any object accelerate). When you are selecting the context, you want to choose a context that will be accessible to your students. The context may be based on an investigation(s) that the students completed in class, which would provide all students with a common experience. On the other hand, you may choose to have students write a scientific explanation around secondhand data (i.e., data someone else collected perhaps from a book or on the Internet). In this case, the context should include a phenomenon with which the students will be familiar. For example, if you live in an area of the country where it never snows, you would not want to use downhill skiing as an example for exploring friction.

In terms of writing versus talk, both ways of communicating are essential for elementary students. Selecting the form of communication you will use will depend on your goals for your students as well as your students' experiences with talk and writing. You may also decide you want to alternate using the different forms over the course of the year in order to provide students with experience and opportunities with both talk and writing as well as to provide you with different ways to assess their understanding.

Fourth-Grade Writing Case: Assessment Task

In Ms. Robinson's case, she developed a formative assessment task in the middle of a unit on force and motion. Unpacking of the content standard helped her specify that the key learning goal for the assessment was that the larger the force, the greater the change in motion in terms of speed or direction. Specifically, the curriculum she used focused on speed, so she wanted her students to understand that a greater force can cause an object to move faster. In terms of the variation of the framework, Ms. Robinson had been using Variation #3 in her class. Therefore, she wanted the assessment item to include the opportunity for students to provide a claim justified by multiple pieces of evidence and reasoning that explained why their evidence supported their claim. The learning performance specified what counted as evidence and reasoning for the force and motion content. In terms of context, Ms. Robinson wanted to assess her students' abilities to construct a scientific explanation about the results of an investigation they completed exploring the motion of a car. The students changed the force applied to a car and recorded observations about the car's motion. Finally, Ms. Robinson wanted to focus on her fourth-grade students' writing. Writing across the content areas was a focus in her school and she wanted to help her students become better science writers. Figure 6.3 describes the investigation the students completed as well as the writing prompt.

FIGURE 6.3

Force and Motion Assessment Task

Students built vehicles that looked like the following:

In this investigation, the string on the end of the car is attached to washers that hang off the table. The weight of the washers is directly related to the force that makes the vehicle move. The students change the number of washers hanging off the table to investigate the relationship between the weight of the washers (i.e., the amount of force) and the speed of the vehicle. Specifically, Ms. Robinson asked them to test the vehicle using 2 washers, 4 washers, 8 washers, and 16 washers. After completing the investigation, she gave them the following writing prompt and reminded them to write a scientific explanation that included a claim, evidence, and reasoning:

Does the weight of the washers change the speed of the vehicle?

The wording of the question is fairly structured and guides students to construct one of two possible claims: Either the weight of the washers, which is directly related to the force, does change the speed or the weight does not change the speed. In terms of evidence, Ms. Robinson wanted her students to include multiple pieces of evidence to support their claim. Consequently, when she designed the investigation, she asked her students to conduct four trials with the different numbers of washers. Furthermore, the evidence allowed her to assess whether her students held two common misconceptions about force and motion: (1) Force is the property of the object and (2) motion exists in two categories—moving and not moving. Finally, in terms of reasoning, Ms. Robinson wanted the students to use the science ideas they had been learning in class about force and motion to explain why their evidence supported their claim. The assessment item provided her fourth-grade students the opportunity to show what they had learned both about force and motion as well as scientific explanations.

Third-Grade Podcast Case: Assessment Task

Ms. Sasaki designed her assessment as a summative assessment for the end of a unit on energy and electricity. The unpacking of the electricity standard highlighted the importance of having students understand that a complete circuit (or unbroken loop) is required for a light bulb to light and that some materials allow the movement of electricity whereas others do not. Furthermore, the unpacking highlighted that some students hold the misconception that a light bulb can light if just one side is connected to a battery in a linear fashion. Consequently, Ms. Sasaki was interested to hear her students' ideas during the podcast around how to light a light bulb. In terms of the variation of the framework, she focused on Variation #2 and was looking for her students to provide multiple pieces of evidence for the claim they made during the podcast. The learning performance helped specify what the teacher was looking for in terms of evidence for those claims—observations from their investigations about what materials and configurations allowed the light bulb to light. Finally, she selected having her students develop podcasts to provide them with an opportunity to share what they had learned about energy using science talk, including a focus on using claims and evidence. This also allowed students to use drawings and photos of their investigations as evidence to support their claim. Figure 6.4 illustrates how Ms. Sasaki introduced the assessment to her class during a full-class discussion.

Designing the assessment as a podcast encouraged students to engage in science talk with their peers. The students had to talk to each other to determine what claims to make and how to justify those claims. The students also needed to find ways to show their evidence through the use of photos, drawings, and posters. By making their thinking public (the podcasts were posted to the class website), the podcast encouraged the third-graders to consider their audience and to think about

FIGURE 6.4

Electrical Circuit Assessment Task

Ms. Sasaki used the KLEW chart from the energy unit to introduce the podcast assessment. She had students work in groups with about four students in each group. She asked students to create a podcast to share what they had learned about electricity. Specifically, she encouraged them to work on using the claim statements from the chart ("L"—what they had learned stated as claims) and then to provide evidence for those claims using the investigations they had conducted in class. Specifically, in terms of electricity concepts, she wanted them to make claims about what was needed to create a circuit that would light a light bulb.

how they were going to convince their audience that their claims about circuits were appropriate. This encouraged them to think about the strength of their evidence and what would be most persuasive to someone else. Although the students' discussion often included reasoning, because they applied science ideas to figure out why their evidence supported their claims, this was not a focus of this assignment. Rather, Ms. Sasaki just wanted the students to focus on claims and evidence in their presentations because they were relatively new at this scientific inquiry practice. With more experienced students, the assessment could be expanded to ask students to include not only reasoning but also the rebuttal in the podcast.

Step 5: Develop Specific Rubric

The last step in the assessment process is to develop a rubric using the claim, evidence, and reasoning framework that specifies what you are looking for in the students' responses. We develop the specific rubrics by adapting a base rubric that can be used across different content areas (McNeill et al., 2006; McNeill & Krajcik, 2012). Table 6.5 illustrates the base scientific explanation rubric, which includes the four different components: claim, evidence, reasoning, and rebuttal. In using this base rubric to design the specific rubric, you will decide how many of these components are appropriate for your specific assessment item as well as the level of complexity for each component. In developing the specific rubric, we often begin by creating an ideal student response for the assessment item. This allows us to make explicit expectations for the students in terms of both the framework and the science content. We use both the base rubric and the ideal student response to develop the specific scientific explanation rubric.

In terms of the number of components, the specific rubric may contain two components (claim and evidence), three components (claim, evidence, and reasoning) or four components (claim, evidence, reasoning, and rebuttal). The number depends on the variation of the framework you are using with your students. For each component, the rubric contains multiple levels that are dependent on the specific assessment

TABLE 6.5 Base Rubric for Scientific Explanation

	Claim	Evidence	Reasoning	Rebuttal
	A statement or conclusion that answers the original question/problem.	*Scientific data that support the claim. The data need to be appropriate and sufficient to support the claim.*	*A justification that connects the evidence to the claim. It shows why the data count as evidence by using appropriate and sufficient scientific principles.*	*Recognizes and describes alternative explanations, and provides counterevidence and reasoning for why the alternative explanation is not appropriate.*
LEVEL 0	Does not make a claim, or makes an inaccurate claim.	Does not provide evidence, or only provides inappropriate evidence (evidence that does not support claim).	Does not provide reasoning, or only provides inappropriate reasoning.	Does not recognize that alternative explanation exists and does not provide a rebuttal or makes an inaccurate rebuttal.
Varies from 1 to 5	Makes an accurate but incomplete claim.	Provides appropriate but insufficient evidence to support claim. May include some inappropriate evidence.	Provides reasoning that connects the evidence to the claim. May include some scientific principles or justification for why the evidence supports the claim, but it is not sufficient.	Recognizes alternative explanations and provides appropriate but insufficient counterevidence and reasoning in making a rebuttal.
	Makes an accurate and complete claim.	Provides appropriate and sufficient evidence to support claim.	Provides reasoning that connects the evidence to the claim. Includes appropriate and sufficient scientific principles to explain why the evidence supports the claim.	Recognizes alternative explanations and provides appropriate and sufficient counterevidence and reasoning when making rebuttals.

Source: McNeill & Krajcik (2012), p. 114.

item and the experience of your students. For example, the highest level of the evidence component states, "Provides appropriate and sufficient evidence to support the claim." If your students are relatively new at creating scientific explanations, you may be using Variation #1, in which case one piece of evidence would be considered appropriate and sufficient. If your students are more advanced, you may require them to include multiple pieces of evidence. In this case, the multiple pieces of evidence are determined by the actual data available to students. In some instances, two pieces of evidence may be sufficient, but in other cases, five pieces of evidence may be necessary to have sufficient evidence. The number of levels in the rubric varies depending on the context of the assessment item. Consequently, the maximum number of points in a rubric varies depending on the number of components and the number of levels for each component. For example, the specific rubric may contain two components with three levels for each component (maximum score of 6); four components with two levels for each component (maximum score of 8); or three components with different levels for each, such as two levels for claim, four levels for evidence, and three levels for reasoning (maximum score of 9). We will illustrate this process using the fourth-grade force and motion case and the third-grade electricity case.

Fourth-Grade Writing Case: Rubric

For the fourth-grade force and motion writing assessment, Ms. Robinson expected her students to include three components in their response (claim, evidence, and reasoning) when they were answering the question, *Does the weight of the washers change the speed of the vehicle?* To develop the specific rubric, we began by writing an ideal student response that included these components:

> *The washers change the speed of the vehicle (CLAIM). When we put two washers on the car, it moved slowly from rest and not very far. With four washers, it moved more quickly and farther. With eight washers, it moved even faster and farther. Finally, with sixteen washers it moved the fastest and farthest (EVIDENCE). The weight of the washers was directly related to the force that made the vehicle move. The more washers we added, the more force we added. The more force we added, the faster and farther the vehicle traveled (REASONING).*

Next, we combined the ideal student response with the base rubric to determine the number of components, the levels of each component, and the specific science content that we wanted the students to include in their response. Table 6.6 includes the specific rubric for this assessment item.

Claim. The wording of the question is fairly structured and encourages students to provide one of two claims: Either the washers did not change the speed of the vehicle or the washers did change the speed of the vehicle. But students may also

TABLE 6.6 Specific Rubric for Force and Motion Investigation

	Claim	Evidence	Reasoning
	A statement or conclusion that answers the original question/problem.	*Scientific data that supports the claim. The data need to be appropriate and sufficient to support the claim.*	*A justification that connects the evidence to the claim. It shows why the data count as evidence by using appropriate and sufficient scientific principles.*
0	Does not make a claim, or makes an inaccurate claim like "The washers do not change the speed of the vehicle."	Does not provide evidence, or only provides inappropriate evidence or vague evidence, like "The data show me it is true" or "Our investigation is the evidence."	Does not provide reasoning, or only provides inappropriate reasoning like "Nothing moved."
1	Makes an accurate but vague claim like "Yes."	Provides 1 of the following 4 pieces of evidence: • Two washers moved slow (or did not move). • Four washers moved faster or farther. • Eight washers moved even faster or farther. • Sixteen moved the fastest or farthest. May also include inappropriate evidence.	Provides 1 of the following 2 reasoning components: • The weight of the washers was directly related to the force that made the vehicle move. • The more washers added (or the more force), the faster or farther the vehicle moved.
2	Makes an accurate and complete claim like "The washers do change the speed of the vehicle."	Provides 2 of the following 4 pieces of evidence: • Two washers moved slow (or did not move). • Four washers moved faster or farther. • Eight washers moved even faster or farther. • Sixteen moved the fastest or farthest. May also include inappropriate evidence.	Provides 2 of the following 2 reasoning components: • The washers were the force on the vehicle. • The more washers added (or the more force), the faster or farther the vehicle moved.
3		Provides 3 of the following 4 pieces of evidence: • Two washers moved slow (or did not move). • Four washers moved faster or farther. • Eight washers moved even faster or farther. • Sixteen moved the fastest or farthest. May also include inappropriate evidence.	
4		Provides all 4 pieces of evidence: • Two washers moved slow (or did not move). • Four washers moved faster or farther. • Eight washers moved even faster or farther. • Sixteen moved the fastest or farthest. It does not include any inappropriate evidence.	

provide a vague claim. Consequently, the rubric includes three levels (0, 1, and 2). Students receive a Level 2 for making an accurate and complete claim, such as "The washers do change the speed of the vehicle." They receive a Level 1 for making a vague claim, such as "Yes." And finally, students receive a Level 0 if they do not provide a claim or provide an inaccurate claim.

Evidence. For evidence, there are four different pieces of evidence the students should include in their written response. When the students completed the investigation, they tested the motion of the vehicle using two, four, eight, and sixteen washers. The students' evidence should include observations about the motion of the vehicle for each of these four cases. Consequently, the rubric includes five levels (0, 1, 2, 3, and 4). Students receive a Level 4 if they discuss their observations for the vehicle using two, four, eight, and sixteen washers, including that each increase in washers resulted in the vehicle traveling farther and faster. If they discuss some of their observations but not all, they receive the corresponding level in the middle (i.e., 1, 2 or 3). For example, if they discuss the results from two washers and four washers but none of the others, they would receive a Level 2. Students receive a Level 0 if they include no evidence or vague evidence, such as writing "The data show me it is true."

Reasoning. In the reasoning, the students must explain why their evidence supports their claim, using the science ideas they had learned about in class about force. The rubric includes three different levels for reasoning (i.e., 0, 1, or 2). Students receive the highest level if they include two components in their reasoning: (1) The weight of the washers was directly related to the force on the vehicle and (2) The more washers added (or the more force), the faster or farther the vehicle traveled. Including both components illustrates not only that the students understood that adding the washers changed the motion of the car but also that this occurred because the washers were acting as a force on the car. If the students discuss only one of these two components, they receive a Level 1. Students receive a Level 0 if they do not provide any reasoning or only provide inappropriate reasoning like writing that "nothing moved."

In developing the rubric for this assessment, we debated the level of detail and complexity that should be included in the rubric. For example, in terms of evidence, the rubric could be more complex if it required that the students include specific measurements for the motion of the car (e.g., with two washers, the car traveled 36 centimeters). In this case, Ms. Robinson decided that the students would only be required to include general observations about the changes, and not specific measurements, in order to focus the students on the overarching trend. Yet in another teacher's classroom, it may be important for the students to include the specific measurements. When designing rubrics, you will need to make numerous decisions, which will be dependent on the backgrounds and experiences of your particular students.

Third-Grade Podcast Case: Rubric

For the third-graders' podcasts, they were asked to provide multiple pieces of evidence to support their claim about what is required to light a light bulb. Consequently, both the ideal response and the rubric focus on two components: claim and evidence. Because this example asks students to develop a podcast, it is actually challenging to write an ideal response in text. However, here we attempt to describe what an ideal response would look like in a podcast:

> *A complete circuit is required to light a light bulb (CLAIM). The evidence includes drawings and photos of the investigations, which show the four different ways that students were able to light the light bulb. All four ways should include a complete circle with one wire, one incandescent bulb, and one battery. The configuration of the materials varies for the four examples: (1) bottom of the bulb on the positive end of the battery and wire on the side of the bulb leading to the negative end of the battery, (2) side of the bulb on the positive end of the battery and wire on the bottom of the bulb leading to the negative end of the battery, (3) bottom of the bulb on the negative end of the battery and wire on the side of the bulb leading to the positive end of the battery, and (4) side of the bulb on the negative end of the battery and wire on the bottom of the bulb leading to the positive end of the battery. (EVIDENCE)*

We then combined this ideal response with the base rubric in order to develop a specific rubric. Table 6.7 includes the specific rubric for the electricity podcast.

Claim. In the podcast, the students needed to make a claim about what is required to light a light bulb. An accurate and complete claim would include a statement about how a complete circuit or a complete circle is required to light a light bulb. Students can also make a vague claim in which they express the importance of connecting the materials, but it is not clear if they understand that this needs to occur in a complete circle. Consequently, the rubric includes three levels—Level 2 is accurate and complete, Level 1 is accurate and vague and Level 0 is either no claim or an inaccurate claim. For example, a Level 2 claim might say, "A complete circuit is required to light a bulb" while a Level 1 claim might state, "We got the bulb to light by connecting the wire to the battery." In the Level 1 example, it is not clear that the students understand that the materials need to be connected in a complete circuit.

Evidence. For evidence, students needed to provide four pieces of evidence to support their claim. In contrast to the fourth-grade force and motion example, this evidence was not solely focused on words, but rather required the use of drawings and photos to illustrate how the materials in the circuit were connected to support the claim that a complete circuit is required to light a bulb. During the students'

	Claim	Evidence
	A statement or conclusion that answers the original question/problem.	*Scientific data that supports the claim. The data needs to be appropriate and sufficient to support the claim.*
0	Does not make a claim, or makes an inaccurate claim like "All you need is a light bulb."	Does not provide evidence, or only provides inappropriate evidence or vague evidence, like "The data show me it is true" or "Our investigation is the evidence."
1	Makes an accurate but vague claim like "We got the bulb to light by connecting the wire to the battery."	Provides 1 of 4 pieces of evidence using drawings and photos. All four ways should include a complete circle with one wire, one bulb, and one battery: • bottom of the bulb on the positive end of the battery and wire on the side of the bulb leading to the negative end of the battery, • side of the bulb on the positive end of the battery and wire on the bottom of the bulb leading to the negative end of the battery, • bottom of the bulb on the negative end of the battery and wire on the side of the bulb leading to the positive end of the battery, and • side of the bulb on the negative end of the battery and wire on the bottom of the bulb leading to the positive end of the battery May also include inappropriate evidence.
2	Makes an accurate and complete claim like "A complete circuit is required to light a bulb."	Provides 2 of 4 pieces of evidence using drawings and photos. All four ways should include a complete circle with one wire, one bulb, and one battery: • bottom of the bulb on the positive end of the battery and wire on the side of the bulb leading to the negative end of the battery, • side of the bulb on the positive end of the battery and wire on the bottom of the bulb leading to the negative end of the battery, • bottom of the bulb on the negative end of the battery and wire on the side of the bulb leading to the positive end of the battery, and • side of the bulb on the negative end of the battery and wire on the bottom of the bulb leading to the positive end of the battery May also include inappropriate evidence.
3		Provides 3 of 4 pieces of evidence using drawings and photos. All four ways should include a complete circle with one wire, one bulb, and one battery: • bottom of the bulb on the positive end of the battery and wire on the side of the bulb leading to the negative end of the battery, • side of the bulb on the positive end of the battery and wire on the bottom of the bulb leading to the negative end of the battery, • bottom of the bulb on the negative end of the battery and wire on the side of the bulb leading to the positive end of the battery, and • side of the bulb on the negative end of the battery and wire on the bottom of the bulb leading to the positive end of the battery May also include inappropriate evidence.
4		Provides 4 of 4 pieces of evidence using drawings and photos. All four ways should include a complete circle with one wire, one bulb, and one battery: • bottom of the bulb on the positive end of the battery and wire on the side of the bulb leading to the negative end of the battery, • side of the bulb on the positive end of the battery and wire on the bottom of the bulb leading to the negative end of the battery, • bottom of the bulb on the negative end of the battery and wire on the side of the bulb leading to the positive end of the battery, and • side of the bulb on the negative end of the battery and wire on the bottom of the bulb leading to the positive end of the battery

TABLE 6.7 Specific Rubric for Electrical Circuit Podcast

investigations, they collected data that four different configurations would result in the lighting of the light bulb: (1) bottom of the bulb on the positive end of the battery and wire on the side of the bulb leading to the negative end of the battery, (2) side of the bulb on the positive end of the battery and wire on the bottom of the bulb leading to the negative end of the battery, (3) bottom of the bulb on the negative end of the battery and wire on the side of the battery leading to the positive end of the battery, and (4) side of the bulb on the negative end of the battery and wire on the bottom of the battery leading to the positive end of the battery. Consequently, the rubric includes five different levels (Levels 0-4), depending on how many of these pieces of evidence the students incorporated into their podcast.

In developing the specific rubric, we debated how much detail the students need to include in their evidence. Specifically, we questioned whether the students should include both a drawing *and* a photo for each configuration or if they needed only to include either a drawing *or* a photo for each configuration to receive the highest level in the rubric. Because Ms. Sasaki had encouraged the third-graders to include both in their podcasts, we decided to require both drawings and a photo for each piece of evidence. Yet, as we mentioned previously, the level of specificity in the rubric is really dependent on your knowledge of your students and how you structure the assessment. There are multiple decisions and trade-offs you need to consider in their development.

Using Assessment Data to Inform Instruction

Although assessments are often considered narrowly, such as in terms of high-stakes standardized tests, assessment data can actually serve multiple purposes in your classroom instruction (NRC, 2001). Specifically, we focus on three purposes of assessment data: (1) making student thinking visible, (2) providing students with feedback, and (3) modifying future instruction. When students construct scientific explanations in either writing or talk, the explanations provide you with a window into student thinking. This enables you to develop an understanding of students' strengths and weaknesses in terms of both the science content and scientific explanations. Providing students with feedback on these strengths and weaknesses can help all students develop a stronger understanding. Furthermore, you can use this information to modify your instruction to better meet the needs of your students in the future.

Fourth-Grade Writing Case: Examples

In evaluating her students' writing, overall Ms. Robinson was pleased with the results. All of her fourth-graders were able to construct an accurate and complete claim about the impact of the washers on the speed of the vehicle. Furthermore, all of the students included some evidence, although Ms. Robinson still found that the evidence was not always complete. Furthermore, as we mentioned in Step 2 of the assessment development process, Ms. Robinson had found that her students struggled with including scientific ideas and language in their reasoning when they

133

Using
Assessment
Data to
Inform
Instruction

were explaining how or why their evidence supported their claim. Consequently, during this lesson, she focused on supporting students in their reasoning. Overall, in assessing the students' writing, she was pleased to see that the majority of the students were discussing the ideas of force and motion, though again some of the students' reasoning was incomplete. We will discuss two examples to illustrate the challenges some students still had with their writing.

Fourth-Grade Example with Incomplete Evidence and Incomplete Reasoning Figure 6.5 includes an example from a student who struggled with both evidence and reasoning. In this example, Louisa makes the correct claim, "Yes the weight of the washers change the speed of the vehicle." Consequently, using the rubric (see Table 6.6), we gave her a score of 2 out of the 2 levels. In terms of evidence, Louisa only specifically discusses the results when she investigated the effect of eight washers and sixteen washers. She does not describe what occurred when she tested the vehicle with either two washers or four washers. Consequently, she receives a Level 2 out of 4 for discussing two pieces of evidence. In terms of feedback, specific comments or questions about her evidence may help Louisa provide a stronger justification for her claim; for example: *You do a nice job providing evidence about what happened with eight washers and sixteen washers. What specifically did you observe with two and four washers?*

Finally, in terms of reasoning, Louisa does describe that the more washers, the faster the vehicle will travel. Specifically, she writes: "Newton's law states the more weight you put on the car, the faster it goes." Although she does bring in the phrase "Newton's law," Louisa does not explicitly make the connection that the weight

FIGURE 6.5

Fourth-Grade Example with Incomplete Evidence and Reasoning

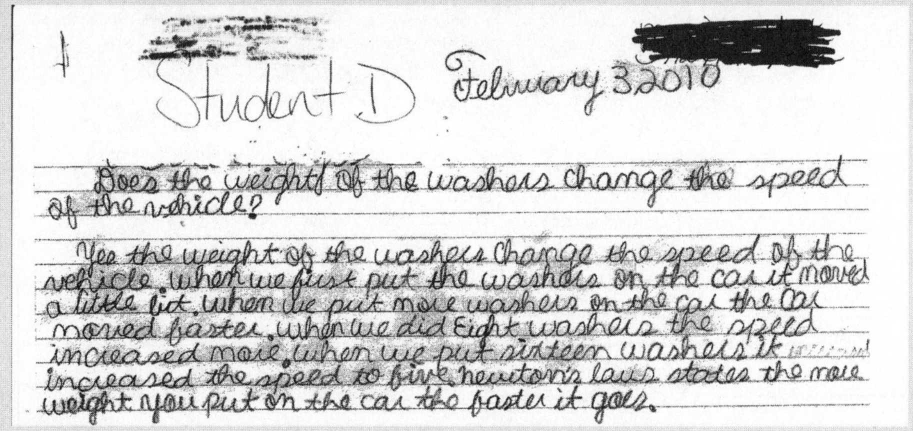

of the washers is directly related to the force that makes the car move; rather, she talks only about weight. Consequently, for reasoning, she receives a Level 1 out of 2. Feedback could focus on incorporating the idea of force into her writing; for example *You are correct that the more weight, the more the car's speed changes. You should also specifically talk about how force impacts the speed of the car. What acted as the force in your investigation?* Overall, Louisa includes some appropriate evidence and reasoning to support her claim, but her scientific explanation is just not complete.

Fourth-Grade Example with Incomplete Evidence and Complete Reasoning. The second fourth-grade example from Akani in Figure 6.6 illustrates a student who provides a stronger justification for the claim but still has incomplete evidence. Similar to Louisa, he also makes the correct claim, "Yes the weight of the washers changes the speed of the vehicle." Consequently, he also receives a Level 2 for his claim. In terms of evidence, he discusses what occurred during the investigation with two, four, and eight washers; however, he leaves out a description of the results with sixteen washers. Because he discusses three of the four pieces of evidence, he received a Level 3. Providing Akani with feedback could focus on including that last piece of evidence—for example *You include three excellent pieces of*

FIGURE 6.6

Fourth-Grade Example with Inappropriate Reasoning

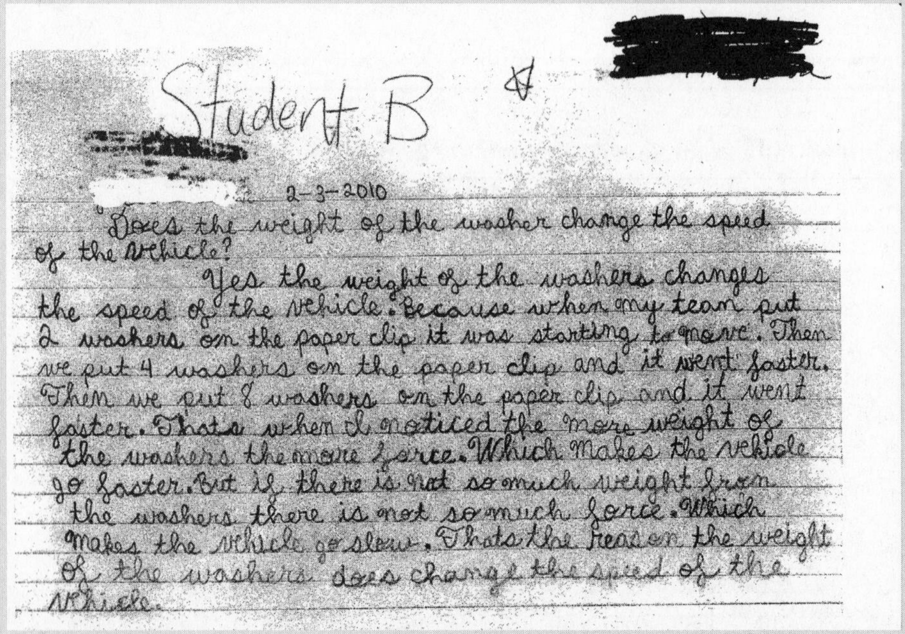

evidence about what occurred with two, four, and eight washers. But what did you observe with sixteen washers? Including one more piece of evidence would make your scientific explanation even stronger.

Finally, in terms of reasoning, Akani received a Level 2 out of 2, because he does make an explicit link between the weight of the washers and force. Specifically, he includes in his reasoning, "That's when I noticed the more weight of the washers the more force. Which makes the vehicle go faster. But if there is not so much weight from the washers there is not so much force. Which makes the vehicle go slow. That's the reason the weight of the washers does change the speed of the vehicle." Although Akani has some difficulty with punctuation, the substance of his reasoning is very strong. He clearly articulates why his evidence supports his claim, including using the concept of force.

Overall, Ms. Robinson was happy with her students' written scientific explanations. The fourth-graders did a nice job justifying their claims with both evidence and reasoning. The students were also more successful than they had been in the past in incorporating the scientific language and science ideas in their writing. The more common difficulty in this assessment was including all four pieces of relevant evidence. Consequently, in the future it would be important to stress that students include all of the evidence available to them to justify their claim.

Third-Grade Podcast Case: Example

Ms. Sasaki's students successfully created podcasts demonstrating what they learned during their investigations of electrical circuits. Observe the podcast 6.1 (0:00–4:23) from one group of four students. During this podcast, the students make an appropriate and complete claim and successfully provide four pieces of evidence to support their claim. They provide the evidence from their investigations before articulating an explicit claim. The students illustrate the four different pieces of evidence in three ways. First, the podcast includes their drawings of the four ways to light a bulb from their investigation (1:00–1:05). Then the students discuss each of the four ways in more detail, including a photo from the investigation and then providing a labeled poster that illustrated the results (1:00–2:11). For example, they describe the first way in stating, "One way it worked was to have the battery standing up with the positive side up. The bottom of the bulb was touching the positive side and one side of the wire was touching the metal ridges while the other side was touching the negative side of the battery." As this is described, both the photo and then the poster are displayed in the podcast. The students include a similar process for the three other ways. Because the students provide both drawings and photos for all four pieces of evidence, they received a 4 out of 4 for evidence.

After describing the results from their investigations, the students then explicitly provide a claim and summarize their evidence. Figure 6.7 includes the transcript from this part of the podcast. The students make a complete and accurate claim, "It

FIGURE 6.7

Third-Grade Example

A: ...so what can you say about creating a circuit and lighting a bulb?

B: We found that it takes a complete circuit to light up a bulb.

A: Scientist Hannah Kurtz, what is your evidence to support that claim?

H: Our evidence is when we connected the battery, bulb, and wire, the bulb lit up. Remember it's important to make sure both the bottom of the bulb and the metal ridges are connected and a part of the circuit!

takes a complete circuit to light up the bulb." Consequently, the students receive a Level 2 of 2 for their claim.

Scientist Kurtz, one of the students in the podcast, goes on to summarize the evidence that Ms. Sasaki's students had provided for their claim. Since Ms. Sasaki did not ask the students to include reasoning, we did not score the students' podcast for this component. However, this summary of the evidence at the end does include some reasoning for why the evidence supports the claim in terms of the importance of connecting both the bottom of the bulb and the metal ridges. Overall, the students were very successful in justifying their claim with appropriate evidence.

Assessing Informal Science Talk

Throughout this chapter, we discuss the development of assessment questions and rubrics for student writing as well as more formal science talk contexts such as a podcast. The claim, evidence, and reasoning framework can also be used to assess students' understanding in more informal science talk situations. In particular, this can be beneficial for evaluating students' understanding in the early grades, such as kindergarten and first grade, when writing and other formal contexts can be more challenging for students. Kindergarten and primary teachers often use informal assessments particularly since their students may not be receiving formal science grades. These informal assessments allow teachers to obtain insights into students' learning and understanding of the explanation building process (Settlage & Sutherland, 2007).

Video clip 6.1 shows an interview with Mrs. Kur in which she discusses how she uses claims and evidence to assess her first-grade students during science talk. She explains that because first-graders are not able to write in detail about their understanding, she uses science talks as a critical tool for assessing her students. Listening as the students work in small groups or with a partner is an important part of how Mrs. Kur knows whether her students are able to make claims and use evidence to support their claims. After her students have explored and tested phenomena,

VIDEO 6.1
Assessment in First Grade

Mrs. Kur talks about gathering the class together for a science talk. She shares that the talk helps her to put together the whole picture of who is really able to look at the question for the day and provide an answer and then support that answer with evidence. Early in the school year, Mrs. Kur says she chooses to introduce the term *claim* as the answer to the question the children are working on, and *evidence* as the way they know the answer. She explains that the first-graders clearly enjoy using words such as *claim* and *evidence* because they want to think and act like scientists. In addition, Mrs. Kur believes her young students are able to handle using these words accurately.

As part of the science talk, Mrs. Kur comments that she asks her students to show their evidence. She explains that as part of the talk, she brings in a set of materials that the students have used in their investigations, and students show what they observed as evidence to support their claims. The use of observable materials helps students who might be struggling with English proficiency to be able to watch and show what they have learned. In addition, the demonstration with the materials provides repetition of what happened in the investigation for learners who need to see things several times before the concepts are retained. As Mrs. Kur narrates how she encourages her students to agree or disagree with the claims or evidence of other students, she explains that she does not allow them to agree or disagree without adding a "because" to further justify their response. When she discusses the process of class construction of claims and evidence, she says that the class listens to several ideas and evaluates together which one makes the best claim. Mrs. Kur encourages students to try to put the claims and evidence into sentences. After the class agrees on those ideas, she often then records them on a KLEW chart as an observable record for the whole class.

In the second part of the video clip, Mrs. Kur discusses using a science conference as another way to assess her students' understanding at the end of a unit. Her description is similar to the vignette from Mr. Garcia at the beginning of the chapter. She notes that units where the class had fully developed a KLEW chart such as magnets, light, or sound are particularly effective for this type of assessment. The students work in partners to use claims and evidence from the class KLEW chart to share at the conference. The classroom is set up with a table and signs, and the children sit audience style and wear their lab coats (white shirts from Goodwill). In addition, Mrs. Kur video records the conference and puts it on DVDs for the parents of the students to see and understand the science content and the extent of the students' understanding of the content. Consequently, the science conference provides the teacher with an opportunity to assess the students' understanding of the science content and scientific explanations. The teacher is also able to provide parents with a record of the students' science talk. This is an important form of assessment that allows students to demonstrate using talk and investigation materials to illustrate what they have learned during the science unit.

Check Point

In this chapter, we described a five-step process for developing scientific explanation assessment tasks: (1) identify and unpack the content standards, (2) select the scientific explanation level of complexity, (3) create a learning performance, (4) write the assessment task, and (5) develop a specific rubric. This process enables you to develop assessments that align with the key science content and scientific explanation learning goals for your students. Furthermore, using the rubrics to analyze student work can help make student thinking visible, provide students with feedback, and modify your future instruction to better meet the needs of students. Finally, we describe how the claims, evidence, and reasoning framework can serve as an important assessment tool during more informal science talk situations to evaluate student learning. In the final chapter, we discuss how to create a classroom community of young scientists that prioritizes the role of using evidence and reasoning to support claims.

Study Group Questions

1. Select a standard for your science curriculum and create an assessment task using the five steps for the development process.

   a. What alternative conceptions might your students have about the science content?

   b. Why did you select the scientific explanation level of complexity for your specific assessment task?

   c. Give the assessment task to a colleague and ask her or him to write an ideal student response. How is your colleague's response similar and different from the one you wrote? Considering the response, do you think you need to revise the assessment item at all?

2. Use a specific rubric to analyze your students' writing or science talk (such as a podcast). What strengths and weaknesses did you observe? How could you use this information to inform your future instruction?

3. Use the scientific explanation framework to assess students' level of understanding of both the content and the scientific explanation practice during an informal science talk. What strengths and weaknesses did you observe with your students?

Fostering a Community of Young Scientists over Time

As a teacher, how can you create a classroom community in which students think, talk, and write scientifically? How can students be involved in shaping the norms of participation in their science learning community? How can you support your own journey as a teacher in order to improve your practice over time? In the following vignette from Mrs. Kur's first-grade class, consider how she helps students create expectations for productive participation to foster a community of young scientists.

Mrs. Kur began the school year with a science talk in which she and her students talked about what scientists do. She asked her students, "What do you call somebody who does science?" One boy responded by saying, "I do science," and then went on to tell a story about using a kit to look at germs under a microscope. Mrs. Kur observed that she heard him saying science

140

Fostering A
Community
Of Young
Scientists
Over Time

involves looking at things and using science tools like microscopes. Since none of the students used the word scientist *to answer her question, Mrs. Kur told them that someone who does science is called a scientist. "Have you heard the word* scientist*?" Many students responded that they had. "Good, because we are going to do lots of science in Room 20 and I want us to learn more about what scientists do and how they act. What do you think scientists do?" One student responded that they study things. "What kinds of things do they study?" queried Mrs. Kur. Students responded with ideas like plants, bugs, dinosaurs, bones, and rocks and minerals. "What does it mean to study?" Mrs. Kur asked the class. One girl explained that it is like working on something, finding out things and then telling other people about it. Another student added that it is discovering new things.*

After this discussion, Mrs. Kur decided to read a book to the students called What Is a Scientist? *The book introduces the idea that scientists ask questions and try to find the answers, they learn with their senses, write things down, make measurements, and share what they learn with others. Mrs. Kur suggested that the class make a list of "What do we want our classroom to be like so we can be scientists?" With some prompting, the students began to list things they wanted to do so the class could be more like a community of scientists. Their list included using tools, making careful observations, sharing ideas and materials, asking questions, listening to what people have to say, and having fun!*

Throughout the year, Mrs. Kur intentionally revisited this list of ideas and added more specifics ideas and examples. For instance, as you saw in Chapter 5 in video clip 5.4 at the beginning of a science talk about solids and liquids, Mrs. Kur reminded her students why listening to one another is so important. She instructed the class to listen carefully because someone might say something you agree with and you will want to support her or him, or someone might say something you disagree with and you'll need to provide reasons why you disagree. Mrs. Kur structured investigations so that students had opportunities to collect and record data to help them construct claims. She used simple claims and evidence charts to help students develop scientific explanations and make sense of their investigations. Her students engaged in scientific talk and practices during each science lesson.

This vignette illustrates how even young children can begin to think of themselves as scientists and engage in scientific practices. Mrs. Kur introduced students to basic practices of science early in the school year, and then built on this foundation as the year progressed, introducing the components of scientific explanation in context. Students were involved in creating a shared vision for their community and determining how members of it would participate. In this way, students have a personal and collective stake in making sure their community functions productively. In this chapter, we focus on the importance of establishing and maintaining a classroom culture that promotes and values social interactions conducive to constructing scientific explanations and making sense of science phenomena. Developing this type of community of young scientists who effectively construct scientific explanations is challenging and can take time. Consequently, we also provide recommendations on how to support your own journey as a science teacher to better support student learning over time.

Norms of Participation in Science Learning

In Chapter 1, we introduced the strands of proficiency for science learning (Duschl et al., 2007; Michaels et al., 2008). At this point, it is important to call attention to the fact that none of the information and ideas we have shared about talking and writing scientific explanations is possible to implement without attending to strand 4: *Participating Productively in Science,* which "calls for students to understand the appropriate norms for presenting scientific arguments and evidence and to practice productive social interactions with peers in the context of classroom science investigations" (Michaels et al., 2008, p. 21). Unfortunately, this is the strand that generally receives minimal attention in school science, particularly in elementary grades. Here our aim is to address the importance of establishing productive talk patterns to support learning science, and return to the framework for scientific explanation and how it can facilitate norms for productive participation in science.

Active Listening and Patterns of Talk

Many challenges are associated with getting young children to participate productively in science talks. Not only do they need to learn how to contribute ideas appropriately but they also must learn to listen to one another and build on each other's ideas, which is emphasized in the Common Core Standards for English Language Arts (Common Core State Standards Initiative, 2010). Notice in the vignette of Mrs. Kur's first-grade class that she addresses listening by using the agree/disagree talk technique described in Chapter 4. More specifically, she encourages active listening by suggesting that students need to understand the point being made so that they can weigh it against their own thinking and agree or disagree. For this purpose, students work to clarify and articulate their own thinking, as well as attempt to understand the reasoning of their peers. This becomes an established way of participating in class discussion, which we refer to as a *norm,* after only a few weeks of the teacher modeling the practice with students. We have observed on numerous occasions that students soon automatically launch into a class discussion by stating, "I disagree with Mark because . . . ." Related to this is prompting

142

Fostering A
Community
Of Young
Scientists
Over Time

students to explicate their reasoning. When teachers regularly ask, "Why do you think that?" and "What is your evidence for that claim?" students learn automatically to include reasoning and evidence in their contributions to discussion.

This kind of talk is a significant departure from the patterns of talk often observed in classrooms and across multiple disciplines. One widely observed discussion pattern is known as *IRE: Initiate–Respond–Evaluate* (Lemke, 1990). In this model, the teacher initiates a question, a student responds, and the teacher evaluates the response. For example, consider this example modified from the opening vignette.

> *(I) Mrs. Kur: What does it mean to study?*
>
> *(R) Student: It's like working on something, to find something out.*
>
> *(E/I) Mrs. Kur: Exactly right. Now, what kinds of things do scientists study?*
>
> *(R) Students: [call out] Bugs. Dinosaurs. Rocks.*
>
> *(E) Mrs. Kur: Yes. Scientists study all of these things by asking questions, making close observations, writing things down, and sharing their ideas with others.*

In the IRE model, the teacher immediately moves from one question to the next, evaluating student responses as she goes. However, this is not what actually happened in the vignette. Mrs. Kur solicits ideas from other students and integrates them as part of the guideline/statement that gets included on the class chart. Using the talk model described in Chapter 4 can help teachers break away from the rigid IRE pattern of classroom discourse, which is dominated by the teacher. Instead, classroom discussion can begin to take the form of multiple students participating and connecting to one another's ideas within a scientific community that works together to construct meaning.

A Culture of Constructive Criticism

In our work with elementary teachers, we have learned that they are frequently concerned about encouraging disagreement in the classroom. A study with preservice elementary teachers revealed that one of the most substantial barriers they overcame in the adoption of a perspective on science teaching that emphasizes evidence and explanation was when they recognized that disagreement could serve as a powerful tool for learning (Zembal-Saul, 2009). Working through the disagreement, whether it is about experimental design or the phrasing of the claim in light of the evidence, requires students to make their thinking visible and engage in sophisticated reasoning. By negotiating consensus, students develop a new and rich understanding of the science ideas and/or practices of science.

Creating a classroom culture in which students feel safe to agree and disagree with one another does not happen by accident—it requires thoughtful, open, and collaborative attention to develop the "rules of the game." In the vignette at the beginning of the chapter and in the video clip description that follows, the teachers discuss with students how they want their science class to be. Students agree on guidelines that are posted in the classroom and are revisited over time in context. The classroom community develops a shared vision for appropriate participation and the students enact it when talking and doing science. One important commitment associated with this kind of community is to foster a culture of critique. In such a culture, it is safe to ask questions and propose changes because the collective goal is to co-construct the most scientifically accurate explanation possible. All members of the community are accountable in this pursuit, and critique becomes the vehicle for making improvements over what any individual member of the community could have accomplished on his or her own.

Notice in video clip 7.1 how Ms. Hershberger uses agree/disagree to promote active listening and support a culture of critique, as well as how elements of the framework for scientific explanation are addressed. Ms. Hershberger asks the class to construct a chart about the "Ways We Want Our Science Class to Be." Prior to this lesson, the class added the following items to the chart: *1. To think and act like scientists. 2. Respect everyone's efforts and mistakes. 3. Take care of materials. 4. Work together. 5. Listen to other people's ideas.* As the clip begins, Ms. Hershberger asks the class to think about why listening is important and if there are things that scientists listen for as another scientist talks. One student suggests that listening is an important way to learn. Another student introduces the idea that some scientists don't agree; he explains that scientists have different ideas about what happened to the dinosaurs and as they listen to the different theories some scientists have changed their minds. Ms. Hershberger prompts the class to list this suggestion as "Listening to see if you agree or disagree." A student shares that you might want to add on to what someone says, and another boy suggests that you should listen to see if the person is saying the same thing and giving lots of details about her or his observations. The teacher adds more information about listening to the chart: *5. Listen to other people's ideas so we can learn, so we can see if we agree or disagree, so we can see if we saw the same thing, and so we can add on.* As Ms. Hershberger finishes writing, a girl suggests the word *evidence*, which clearly excites her teacher. The class discusses what evidence is and adds to the chart: *6. Use evidence to support our ideas (claims).*

VIDEO CLIP 7.1
Shaping a Science Community

144

Fostering A
Community
Of Young
Scientists
Over Time

Ms. Hershberger asks the students what it means to "talk like a scientist," and after some probing the class responds that it means to use specific science words that scientists might use—such as *camouflage, urine, hymenoptera,* and so on. The class concluded by making another addition to the chart: *7. Use scientific words as we describe what we see and do.*

Ms. Hershberger used this kind of introductory discussion to lay the foundation for how science classes, and particularly science talks, would look in her classroom. She intentionally asked the class to think deeply about listening and the kind of listening that would be helpful to promote productive science discussions. When students were asked to think about and help formulate a chart that describes science class, they took ownership in the process of becoming a community of scientists. As they practiced their goals and stated objectives for working and listening like scientists, the students became increasingly comfortable with agreeing and disagreeing with each other. The students quickly learned to base their arguments and points of disagreement using aspects of the CER framework rather than on personal issues. Over time, when students shared their thinking, they automatically included the reasoning behind their remarks. They knew that they were expected to share what was underlying their statements, rather than just a simple "yes/no" or "I agree/disagree."

Supporting Your Own Journey

Developing a community of young scientists who prioritize scientific explanations is challenging. In this final part of the book, we consider why, even though it can be challenging for the most experienced professionals, some teachers are still willing to reconsider their practice and adopt a different approach to science teaching. Furthermore, we provide recommendations for aspects to consider as you continue to reflect on and modify your own instruction as a teacher. We thought it would be fitting to include the voices of practicing teachers who were meeting as part of a professional learning community focused on engaging their K–5 students in talking and writing scientific explanations during the development of this book. Their perspectives on the challenges and rewards of teaching science in this way as well as recommendations for the future are summarized in the text that follows and accompanied by video clips of our conversation with them.

Rewards of Teaching Science as Explanation

To better understand what drives teachers to pursue complex practices associated with engaging students in constructing explanations in science, we sat down with Mrs. Jennifer Cody, Mrs. Elizabeth Cullin, Mrs. Jennifer Grube, Ms. Kimber Hershberger, and Mrs. Judi Kur, and asked them to share their thoughts on some of the rewards of teaching science in this way. In video 7.2, the teachers begin by responding, "It's fun!" Jennifer G. states that teaching this way provides students with "a framework with which to articulate their thinking." She notes that it also gives students a process for articulating and supporting their thinking. In addition, Jennifer talks about the significance of students having a mutual understanding with which to approach their science conversations—something we refer to in this book as *norms of participation.* Judi discusses the connections that students are able to make because "they aren't just doing activities; their lessons have meaning and are intentionally scaffolded so meaning can occur." Jennifer C. shares a story of one girl in her class who disliked science and explains how the student's perspective changed as a result of engaging in science discourse and explanation.

For Jennifer G., another benefit surfaced when the students' own questions coincided with the intended objectives, making the lessons authentic and motivating. Her observations were that the students' engagement increased with this type of ownership. Elizabeth calls it "the buy in" and talks about the ways in which student ownership of the questions and the lessons can aid in building a sense of science community in the classroom. Judi mentions that in many schools students don't really "own what's going on" and that there is power when students have a voice in their science learning.

VIDEO CLIP 7.2
Rewards of Teaching for Explanation

Elizabeth discusses the "ah-ha!" moments that occurred for both teachers and students. She saw power in facilitating students' abilities to know the process scientists go through to answer questions, and she witnessed, firsthand, students applying these skills in other subject areas, including social studies and math. Using science explanation tools, such as providing evidence, picks up on students' own sense of wonder, and Elizabeth notes that students feel empowered to search for answers to their questions. Finally, Jennifer G. explains that there are many challenges associated with teaching science in this way and states that it is not an easy process. However, she asserts that having gone through the process this year with some of her science units, she cannot imagine teaching science any other way. The other teachers are clearly in agreement with her point.

Reflections on Changing Practice

Next, in our conversation with teachers (see video clip 7.3), we asked them to describe their attempts to change their science teaching to engage students in constructing scientific explanations. During their discussion, the teachers describe

146

Fostering A
Community
Of Young
Scientists
Over Time

practices they found challenging but also valuable for fostering a community of young scientists engaged in scientific explanations. The group talks about some productive breakthroughs, as well as some difficulties that they encountered as they implemented new strategies in their classrooms. Elizabeth begins by acknowledging that she still feels she has a long way to go—a sentiment shared by the other teachers. She explains that the content storyline aided her in focusing on testable questions, providing a framework for selecting appropriate activities to use during her teaching. She sees the storyline as a type of roadmap for negotiating a terrain of hands-on activities and to ultimately zero in on the important questions that lead to claims aiding her students in developing a richer, more coherent understanding of the science ideas. Jennifer C. adds on to this by claiming that her own content knowledge increased as she worked on creating and connecting the science storyline with her students. Jennifer G. called the content storyline "a sequential journey through a subject." Both Elizabeth and Jennifer G. articulate that using the storyline clearly helped them go deeper into the content while still addressing the standards.

VIDEO CLIP 7.3
Influence on Teaching Practice

Judi asserts that she is still learning and that it is okay to question what you are doing and to question the curriculum and how you get to the objectives. She believes that questioning is a critical part of looking at your own practice. Helping her first-grade students to understand and work with claims and evidence is an important part of Judi's science teaching. Getting her students to understand and use the claim–evidence language in science discussions enables her students to think and talk like scientists. Judi shared that recently she has used more sentence starter scaffolds to help students with writing claims and evidence. In addition, she has structured more opportunities for her class to collect a variety of data to be able to provide clear evidence for making claims.

Jennifer G. also shares her work on claims. Her emphasis is on coming to understand that her students need to make claims that are based on firsthand interactions with phenomena—what they can directly observe, touch, and record. Jennifer G. and Kimber talk about a birdseed investigation that provided fifth-graders with an opportunity to collect observable data by recording the number of species that ate four different types of birdseed. Jennifer feels that this is a strong example of a time when her students were clearly able to make claims based on the evidence they had collected. The excitement of this study group is evident as they share the ways their science teaching practices have evolved through planning connected lessons based on the CER framework. These teachers have developed a strong and trusting learning community as they work together to discuss their successes and areas for continued growth.

As this conversation highlights, even teachers who have been working on integrating scientific explanations into their classroom within a supportive learning community still feel they have a long way to go. The CER framework and strategies in this book provide you with a tool kit that you can adapt to meet the needs of your particular context—your students, science curriculum, school culture, and district and state context. However, the book does not offer a magic pill or one-size-fits-all solution. Rather, it is important to continuously question and reflect on your own practice in order to better support a community of young scientists over the course of the school year, as well as from one school year to the next. Teaching is a demanding profession. Taking the time to rethink and change your practice is ambitious and can present real challenges, but it can also provide you with significant rewards.

Recommendations

We would like to leave you with some advice from teachers who have been successful at integrating a focus on scientific explanation in their classrooms. Video clip 7.4 captures some of the recommendations the group has for teachers who chose to try some of the ideas presented in this book. They begin by suggesting that it is helpful to start small—do not try to take on everything at once. The teachers believe that it is very important to seek out other colleagues for support, either a teaching partner or professional learning community. Working on the content storyline and discerning good questions is tough to do by yourself, so having a support group is extremely helpful for getting feedback during the planning process. Elizabeth suggests that teachers need to have a good background in the content, but that it is okay not to know everything. Part of the process is working together with the students to investigate the phenomena and the scientific principles that will answer questions about the natural world.

The teachers acknowledge that things will not always go the way you expect, so it is important to be flexible with your thinking and with your time. In other words, you may think a lesson will take an hour, but it may take an hour and a half, because when students are engaged in scientific discourse it can be difficult to know exactly how long the discussion will take. Therefore, the process requires patience and flexibility. Judi also adds that it is important to be patient with students, that there is a learning curve for the children as they enter into scientific talk and writing that may be different from what they have experienced in the past.

VIDEO CLIP 7.4
Recommendations

148

Fostering A
Community
Of Young
Scientists
Over Time

The group concludes by discussing the beginning of the school year and gives suggestions for ways to build a science community and to introduce your students to the vocabulary and norms of science talks. Judi suggests choosing something that will excite students (e.g., observing monarch larvae) so they can learn important skills, such as how to make and record detailed observations that will later become the basis of claims. Elizabeth concludes by describing the process of building understanding of the CER framework and modeling the expectations for different parts of the work. As these teachers' recommendations suggest, there are always areas of your instruction that you could focus on to improve. Furthermore, they highlight the importance of being patient with the process and the students as they engage in scientific discourse. We would like to add that it is important to be patient with *yourself* as you integrate strategies for talking and writing about scientific explanations into your own classroom practice.

Check Point

Developing a classroom culture for science in which students construct and debate claims that they justify with evidence and reasoning takes time. Constructing scientific explanations is a challenging task. Yet, hopefully the multiple examples throughout this book illustrate that it is not only an important but an achievable goal for all elementary students. Throughout the book we have included a variety of strategies and lessons learned that have been successful with the teachers and students with whom we have worked. We hope you now believe that you have a tool kit of resources that you can use to successfully engage your students in scientific explanations as you embark on your own journey to foster a community of young scientists.

Study Group Questions

1. Videotape a lesson in which you engage your students in science talk. Watch the video and examine the pattern of talk. Are there times when the talk is structured more in an IRE pattern? Are there times the talk includes greater student interactions? Why do these variations occur in the discussion?

2. Work with your students to develop a chart for the "rules of the game" for your science community. What rules and norms do you and your students feel are important?

3. Consider how you would like your students' scientific explanations to become more sophisticated over time. What are your goals for the beginning of the school year? The end of the school year? How can you help your students achieve these goals?

4. What are your goals for your own journey as a teacher? What aspects of your practice would you like to focus on changing? Why?

References

Adams, C. M., & Pierce, R. L. (2003). Teaching by tiering: Creating lessons with multiple levels can be an effective method for meeting the needs of all learners. *Science and Children*, 3, 30–34.

American Association for the Advancement of Science. (1990). *Science for all Americans*. New York: Oxford University Press.

American Association for the Advancement of Science. (1993). *Benchmarks for science literacy*. New York: Oxford University Press.

American Association for the Advancement of Science. (2009). *Benchmarks Online*. Retrieved May 14, 2010, http://www.project2061.org/publications/bsl/online/index.php

Appleton, K. (2005). *Elementary science teacher education: International perspectives*. Mahwah, NJ: Lawrence Erlbaum.

Avraamidou, L., & Zembal-Saul, C. (2005). Giving priority to evidence in science teaching: A first-year elementary teacher's specialized knowledge and practice. *Journal of Research in Science Teaching*, 42(9), 965–986.

Barreto-Espino, R. (2009). Teaching science as argument: Prospective elementary teachers' knowledge. Unpublished doctoral dissertation, The Pennsylvania State University, University Park, PA.

Bell, P., & Linn, M. C. (2000). Scientific arguments as learning artifacts: Designing for learning from the web with KIE. *International Journal of Science Education*, 22, 797–817.

Bransford, J., Brown, A., & Cocking, R. (Eds.). (2000). *How people learn: Brain, mind, experience and school*. Washington DC: National Academy Press.

Britsch, S. J., & Heise, K. A. (2006). One mode is not for all: Interpreting how special needs students communicate science knowledge. *Science and Children*, 4, 26–29.

Common Core State Standards Initiative. (2010). Retrieved June 29, 2011, http://www.corestandards.org/the-standards/english-language-arts-standards

Davis, E. A., Petish, D., & Smithey, J. (2006). Challenges new science teachers face. *Review of Educational Research*, 76(4), 607–651.

Driver, R., Guesne, E., & Tiberghien, A. (Eds.). (1985). *Children's ideas in science*. Philadelphia: Open University Press.

Driver, R., Squires, A., Rushworth, P., & Wood-Robinson, V. (1994). *Making sense of secondary science: Research into children's ideas.* London: Routledge.

Duschl, R. A., Schweingruber, H. A., & Shouse, A. W. (Eds.). (2007). *Taking science to school: Learning and teaching science in grade K–8.* Washington DC: National Academy Press.

Echevarria, J., Vogt, M., & Short, D. S. (2008). *Making content comprehensible for English learners: The SIOP Model.* Boston: Pearson, Allyn & Bacon.

Fulton, L., & Campbell, B. (2003). *Science notebooks: Writing about inquiry.* Portsmouth, NH: Heinemann.

Gagnon, M. J., & Abell, S. K. (2009). ELLs and the language of school science. *Science and Children,* 5, 50–51.

Grotzer, T., & Perkins, D. (2005). *Causal patterns in simple circuits: Lessons to infuse into electricity units to enable deeper understanding.* Cambridge, MA: President and Fellows of Harvard College. http://www.cfa.harvard.edu/smg/Website/UCP/resources.html

Hammerness, K., Darling-Hammond, L., Bransford, J., Berliner, D., Cochran-Smith, M., & McDonald, M. (2005). In L. Darling-Hammond & J. Bransford (Eds.), *Preparing teachers for a changing world: What teachers should learn and be able to do.* San Francisco: Jossey-Bass.

Hand, B. (Ed.). (2008). *Science inquiry, argument and language: A case for the science writing heuristic.* Rotterdam, The Netherlands: SensePublishers.

Hand, B., & Keys, C. W. (1999). Inquiry investigation: A new approach to laboratory reports. *Science Teacher,* 66, 27–29.

Harlen, W. (2001). *Primary science: Taking the plunge* (2nd ed.). Portsmouth NH: Heinemann.

Hershberger, K., Zembal-Saul, C., & Starr, M. (2006). Evidence helps the KLW get a KLEW. *Science & Children,* 43(5), 50–53.

Keenan, S. (2004). Reaching English language learners: Strategies for teaching science in diverse classrooms. *Science and Children,* 2, 49–51.

Krajcik, J., McNeill, K. L., & Reiser, B. (2008). Learning-goals-driven design model: Curriculum materials that align with national standards and incorporate project-based pedagogy. *Science Education,* 92(1), 1–32.

Krajcik, J. S., & Sutherland, L. (2009). IQWST Materials: Meeting the Challenges of the 21st Century. Paper presented at the NRC workshop on exploring the intersection between science education and the development of 21st century skills.

Kur, J., & Heitzmann, M. (2008, January). Attracting student wonderings: Magnets pull students into scientific inquiry. *Science and Children,* 28–32.

Lee, O. (2005). Science education with English language learners: Synthesis and research agenda. *Review of Educational Research,* 75(4), 491–530.

Lemke, J. (1990). *Talking science: Language, learning and values.* Norwood, NJ: Ablex.

McNeill, K. L. (2011). Elementary students' views of explanation, argumentation and evidence and abilities to construct arguments over the school year. *Journal of Research in Science Teaching*.

McNeill, K. L. (2009). Teachers' use of curriculum to support students in writing scientific arguments to explain phenomena. *Science Education*, 93(2), 233–268.

McNeill, K. L., & Knight, A. M. (in review). Teachers' pedagogical content knowledge of scientific argumentation: The impact of professional development on teaching K–12 science.

McNeill, K. L., & Krajcik, J. (2007). Middle school students' use of appropriate and inappropriate evidence in writing scientific explanations. In M. Lovett & P. Shah (Eds.), *Thinking with data* (pp. 233–265). New York: Taylor & Francis.

McNeill, K. L., & Krajcik, J. (2008a). Scientific explanations: Characterizing and evaluating the effects of teachers' instructional practices on student learning. *Journal of Research in Science Teaching*, 45(1), 53–78.

McNeill, K. L., & Krajcik, J. (2008b). Assessing middle school students' content knowledge and reasoning through written scientific explanations. In J. Coffey, R. Douglas, & C. Stearns (Eds.), *Assessing science learning: Perspectives from research and practice* (pp. 101–116). Arlington, VA: National Science Teachers Association Press.

McNeill, K. L., & Krajcik, J. (2009). Synergy between teacher practices and curricular scaffolds to support students in using domain specific and domain general knowledge in writing arguments to explain phenomena. *Journal of the Learning Sciences*, 18(3), 416–460.

McNeill, K. L., & Krajcik, J. (2012). *Supporting grade 5–8 students in constructing explanations in science: The claim, evidence and reasoning framework for talk and writing*. Boston: Pearson.

McNeill, K. L., Lizotte, D. J., Krajcik, J., & Marx, R. W. (2006). Supporting students' construction of scientific explanations by fading scaffolds in instructional materials. *Journal of the Learning Sciences*, 15(2), 153–191.

McNeill, K. L., & Martin, D. M. (2011). Claims, evidence and reasoning: Demystifying data during a unit on simple machines. *Science and Children*, 48(8), 52–56.

McNeill, K. L., & Pimentel, D. S. (2010). Scientific discourse in three urban classrooms: The role of the teacher in engaging high school students in argumentation. *Science Education*. 94(2), 203–229.

Metz, K. E. (2000). Young children's inquiry in biology: Building the knowledge bases to empower independent inquiry. In J. Minstrell & E. H. van Zee (Eds.), *Inquiring into inquiry learning and teaching in science* (pp. 371–404). Washington, DC: American Association for the Advancement of Science.

Michaels, S., Shouse, A. W., & Schweingruber, H. A. (2008). *Ready, set, science! Putting research to work in K–8 science classrooms*. Board on Science Education, Center for Education, Division of Behavioral and Social Sciences and Education. Washington DC: The National Academy Press.

National Academies. (2009). *Workshop: Exploring the intersection of science education and the development of 21st century skills.*

National Research Council. (1996). *National science education standards*. Washington DC: National Academy Press.

National Research Council. (2000). *Inquiry and the national science education standards: A guide for teaching and learning*. Washington DC: National Academy Press.

National Research Council. (2001). *Classroom assessment and the national science education standards*. Washington DC: National Academy Press.

National Science Resources Center. (2003). *Science and technology for children: Motion and design*. Burlington, NC: Carolina Biological Supply Company.

Nelson, V. (2010). Learning English, learning, science: How science notebooks can help English language learners with two subjects. *Science and Children*, 3, 48–51.

Norton-Meier, L., Hand, B., Hockenberry, L., & Wise, K. (2008). *Questions, claims and evidence: The important place of argument in children's science writing*. Portsmouth, NH: Heinemann.

Ogle, D. M. (1986). K-W-L: A teaching model that develops active reading of expository text. *The Reading Teacher*, 39(6), 564–570.

Olson, J. K., Levis, J. M., Vann, R., & Bruna, K. R. (2009). Enhancing science for ELLs: Science strategies for English language learners that benefit all students. *Science and Children*, 5, 46–48.

Pray, L., & Monhardt, R. (2009). Sheltered instruction techniques for ELLs: Ways to adapt science inquiry lessons to meet the academic needs of English language learners, *Science and Children*, 7, 34–38.

Rose, D. H., & Meyer, A. (2002). *Teaching every student in the Digital Age: Universal Design for Learning*. Alexandria, VA: ASCD.

Roth, K., Chen, C., Lemmens, M., Garnier, H., Wickler, N., Atkins, L., Calabrese Barton, A., Roseman, J. E., Shouse, A., & Zembal-Saul, C. (2009, April). Coherence and science content storylines in science teaching: Evidence of neglect? Evidence of effect? Colloquium and paper presented at the annual meeting of the National Association for Research in Science Teaching (NARST). Garden Grove, CA.

Roth, K., Garnier, H., Chen, C., Lemmens, M., Schwille, K., & Wickler, N.I.Z. (2011). Videobased lesson analysis: Effective Science PD for teacher and student learning. *Journal of Research in Science Teaching*, 48(2), 117–148.

Roth, K. J., Druker, S. L., Garnier, H., Lemmens, M., Chen, C., Kawanaka, T., Rasmussen, D., Trubacova, S., Warvi, D., Okamoto, Y., Gonzales, P., Stigler, J., & Gallimore, R. (2006). Teaching science in five countries: Results from the TIMSS 1999 video study (NCES 2006-2011). Washington DC: National Center for Education Statistics. Available at http://nces.ed.gov/timss

Settlage, J., & Southerland, S. A. (2007). *The nature of science teaching science to every child: Using culture as a starting point*. New York: Taylor & Francis.

Steele, M. M. (2007). Science success for students with special needs: Strategies for helping all students master science standards. *Science and Children*, 2, 48–51.

Toulmin, S. (1958). *The uses of argument.* Cambridge, UK: Cambridge University Press.

Zembal-Saul, C. (2005, April). Preservice teachers' understanding of teaching elementary school science as argument. Paper presented at the annual meeting of the National Association for Research in Science Teaching (NARST), Dallas, TX.

Zembal-Saul, C. (2007, August). Evidence and explanation as a lens for learning to teach elementary school science as argument. Paper presented at the European Science Education Research Association (ESERA) meeting, Malmo, Sweden.

Zembal-Saul, C. (2009). Learning to teach elementary school science as argument. *Science Education*, 93(4), 687–719.

Zembal-Saul, C. (2010). *Toward an emphasis on evidence and explanation in K–5 science teaching*. Poster presented at the International Conference of the Learning Sciences, Chicago.

Index